William James Lee

Poems. Adrift and Anchored

William James Lee

Poems. Adrift and Anchored

Reprint of the original, first published in 1875.

1st Edition 2024 | ISBN: 978-3-38538-364-7

Verlag (Publisher): Outlook Verlag GmbH, Zeilweg 44, 60439 Frankfurt, Deutschland
Vertretungsberechtigt (Authorized to represent): E. Roepke, Zeilweg 44, 60439 Frankfurt, Deutschland
Druck (Print): Books on Demand GmbH, In de Tarpen 42, 22848 Norderstedt, Deutschland

Brack Marah's early God doth send
Along the paths Green Elims end.

Marah at first; then Elim palms,
And twelve cool wells, and restful calms!

Grain is stored up in Heavenly Years
We sow down here in pain and tears.

The hopes that fled from out the breast
Sing in the trees in Land of Rest.

And on the hurricane's swift wing.
We mount to Hills where angels sing.

Kind deeds seem shipwrecked to thine eye—
Their anchors drop in far off sky.

I raise my eyes from Marah's pool;
There—there lies Elim, green and cool!

POEMS.

ADRIFT AND ANCHORED.

BY

REV. WILLIAM J. LEE

KANSAS CITY, MO.:

RAMSEY, MILLETT & HUDSON.

1875.

CONTENTS.

CONTENTS.

AFLOAT:
INTRODUCTION.

No stately ships here leave the tranquil shore
To sail the stormless waters, placid, oer ;
        But many a frail, light boat
        I launch and send afloat.

Perhaps no freight of gold or pearls they bear ;
No wealth of " Ormus or of Ind " is here ;
        But many ready hands
        For daily life demands.

The weariness and dreariness afloat,
A drift, or driven in many an open boat,
        Shall touch the Tranquil Shore—
        All dreary driftings oer !

On seas of life with many a changing mood—
Sometimes oer currents little understood—
    Afloat 'neath angry sky·—
    With storm-blasts hurrying by !

Sometimes the rowers buffet adverse waves,
And my frail boats seem sunk in watery graves :
    Then Jesus, close at hand,
    Brings all my boats to land !

My songs afloat, acrest on every sea,
Rise, dip, and fall with human misery ;
    And many a burden bear ;
    And many a daily prayer.

For human hearts are more like skiffs that fill
With angry waves, than ships of master will :
    And many an open seam
    Lets pressing life-waves in !

And up from depths of many a soul the cry
Rings Godward as some angry wave sweeps by,
  Where bitterest waters roll
  Across the human soul.

These human lives meet many an angry storm:—
But each true life shall meet that Sacred Form
  Walking on Galilee
  To still the angry sea!

Afloat each boat alike through light and night:
Through light to night and through the night to
  light;
  Till past the solemn sky
  They touch Eternity.

Oh! may the souls on many a sea afloat,
Adrift or driven, like open, sailless boat,
  Find anchorage all still
  By God's Celestial Hill.

And in from seas where treacherous currents
    sweep
Far out from shore upon the pathless deep,
        Oh! may each boat there cast
        Its anchor sure at last!

Life-boat, or ship—with sail, or toilsome oar,
From dubious waves and seas touch changeless
    shore.
        How motionless they lie—
        No wild storms hurrying by!

Shut in around by Heavenly Hills, how blest
The boats that lie upon that Harbor's breast!
        Afloat—adrift no more—
        But anchored by the Shore.

ADRIFT AND ANCHORED.

"WHEN YE THINK NOT."

LUKE XII:40.

What a hush is in the cloudless,
Soundless, boundless, speechless sky !
Just as if, through all its portals,
Cares were gliding not to mortals—
Just as if men never die !
    Silence reigning—no complaining
Far along God's world of blue !
And the sun keeps on his shining,
Stars are quietly reclining,
    As if cares they never knew.

Yet there are such countless sorrows,
Shifting, drifting, hurrying near,

From these speechless skies descending,

And no messenger befriending—

Warning us of coming fear !

 Not a token ever spoken

To the heart in its repose.

No alarm beats wild commotion

Far along Life's tideless ocean—

 As if Life should never close.

 Yet there presseth every moment

Rigid, frigid, tireless feet.

O my soul, near thee is danger !

Footsteps of unwelcome Stranger

Soon along thy halls will beat.

 In an hour when least thou fearest,

To some treasure held the dearest,

He will come with noise less tread ;

And some soul will pass the portal

Of the Land we call : " Immortal "—
  From these shores forever fled.

  Who can hear the dip of oars,
Dashing, splashing through the night ?
Who can see the Boatman standing
On the deck, to urge his landing
Ere the coming of the light ?
  Swiftly nearing—onward steering,
Soon to touch some human shore ?
Who can see the oars' quick swinging,
Ever nearer, nearer bringing
  Boat from out Forevermore ?

  Touched it shore one early morning :—
Landing, standing where the gleam
Fell athwart a sweet babe sleeping,
And the mother, love-watch keeping—
Picture fair as fairest dream !

Night had ended—morn ascended—
Pushed it off from earthly strand.
When the light down here was breaking,
Angel oars the child was taking

    Swiftly to the Heavenly Land.

    Touched it human shore one noon-day :—
Waking, breaking into life,
Myriad forms in field and meadow :
Sunshine casting shortest shadow ;
Manhood bending to the strife !

    Full of labor and endeavor :
Little thoughts of griefs or fears.
Swiftly came the great wave swelling,
Reaching quick his earthly dwelling—

    Sweeping to the eternal years !

    Then the evening-time came, silent ;
Filling, chilling earth and air.

And, amid the dubious gloaming,
Aged thoughts were idly roaming
O'er the Past, all wondrous fair.

There!---the plashing sound, and dashing
Of that Barge along the shore!
Oh! when earthly cords are riven,
Steers it for the blissful Haven

In the Land Forevermore?

Midnight! All the earth-lights, rayless.
Gladness, sadness,---all is still!
And the sluggish waves slow beating
On the strand where Life is meeting
Death.   The skies and earth are chill.

There!---that sounding, dumb resounding
Dipping of that fated oar!
Now the aged eyes grow dimmer;
Not the faintest earth-lights glimmer

Here along this midnight shore.

2

O my soul, be watchful—prayerful.
Rigid, frigid, tireless feet
Of the never welcome Stranger,
When thou thinkest least of danger,
Soon along thy halls will beat!

Though no motion stir Life's ocean,
Comes a Form towards the shore.
Who can see that Pilot steering?
Who can see that dark Barge nearing?

Who can hear Death's dripping oar?

JEZREEL.

JUDGES, VIII:4.

I.

From Jezreel's fertile valley,
By Gideon's faithful sword
Drawn for the ranks of Israel
At the quick cry of the Lord,
The Midianitish army
Are driven like chaff by wind!
And the Lord's three hundred chosen
Are pressing fast behind!

On, on to far Zarerath—
To Tabbath far they fled,
Till Esdraelon only
Saw the dying and the dead.

On one side rose Gilboa;
On the other Hermon stood;
Before them lay Beth-shean.
Beside the Jordan's flood.

The hosts of Israel gather
From far hills of the North;
And Naphtali, and Asher,
And Manasseh join their force.
And Ephraim fights with Midian
Along the Jordan's wave;
And Gideon still pursuing
With his chosen band, and brave.

Faint from the midnight battle—
Faint from the wearying way—
Still press they over Jordan,
Pursuing swift their prey!
The Lord's great work unfinished,

How shall they stay their hand
Till Amalek and Midian
Are pressed from Israel's land ?

Oh! that was sight worth seeing!
Oh! that was to be true!—
When Gideon and his followers
Did all there was to do!
Weary, but never resting;
Fainting, yet pressing on;
Ne'er turning from the foes of God
Till victory is won!

II.

There's many a Jezreel valley —
Where is Gideon's flashing sword
To leap from out its scabbard
At the quick cry of the Lord?—
Where sins, like hosts of Midian,

Swarm forth on every hand!
Oh! for the sword of Gideon
To drive them from the land!

There's many a Jezreel valley
Within the human soul,
Where noisy camps are pitching,
And taking sure control.
Has the Lord some trusty champion
To fall upon them there,
And rout the soul's vast legions,
And redeem this valley fair?

Oh! that is sight worth seeing,
When soul, like Gideon true,
Arms for the mighty battle,
To do what is to do!
To go at God's quick bidding
Against unnumbered sin;

And in his strength and armor
The fight with Wrong begin!—

To press the foe, though weary;
Pursuing every day;
Seeking nor rest, nor shadow
Along the rocky way;
Until we come to Jordan,
And the land is freed from sin.
Resting will be to-morrow:
To-day the fight begin!

My soul, Time is thy battle;
Sins are thy foes to-day.
Face God-ward! fall upon them!
Rush down into the fray!
Though sometimes sorely beaten,
New strength from God thou 'lt gain.
To-morrow's camping ground will be
Upon the Eternal Plain!

NOT THERE.

How different from this sin soiled Earth
      Must be the Upper Skies!
A land down here of want and barren dearth,
      Where all that's fair soon dies.

In that fair Paradise of God,
      No shivering midnight air;
No foot of Care that Land hath ever trod ;
      No sorrow dwelleth there.

Not there the wild and wintry sea,
      Wrecking our hearts and homes.
Sea-storms in Heavenly Country cannot be,
      And wrecking never comes.

When anchor drops in waters clear
　　Within the Eternal Bay,
Banished forever is all human fear
　　Of drifting far away!

Forebodings have no place—no home
　　Within the Gates on high;
Their dreary waves break off in angry foam
　　Far—far beneath the sky!

No sin is there.　No blight on flowers
　　Celestial, sweet and fair.
Who walks adown the upper, radiant bowers
　　Finds no sin-traces there.

There are no hours of deep distress;
　　No partings ever come;
No weary steps, no spirit loneliness
　　Within the Heavenly Home.

Golgothas are on earth !   In skies,
      Along the golden streets
Of that Fair City where no spirit dies,
      No nodding plumes one meets !

No worms to gnaw, no ruthless sword,
      No battle-shout, no breath
Contagious meet the armies of the Lord ;
      Up there is " no more death."

And God Himself doth wipe all eyes ;
      Weeping is there unknown.
And His broad wings which sweep remotest skies,
      O'er all for safety thrown !

Those Gates shut out all earthly wrong ;
      They shut within, all bliss.
How different then must be the Ransomed Throng
      From men in world like this !

A River runs this side that Land.

    O, human soul, why fear?

Cares, sins, and death here press on every hand—

    No sins—no death up there!

Weigh anchor!　Outward bound, O soul!

    God will take care of thee!

He'll guide thee up to Life's supremest goal—

    Thy Pilot to the Day.

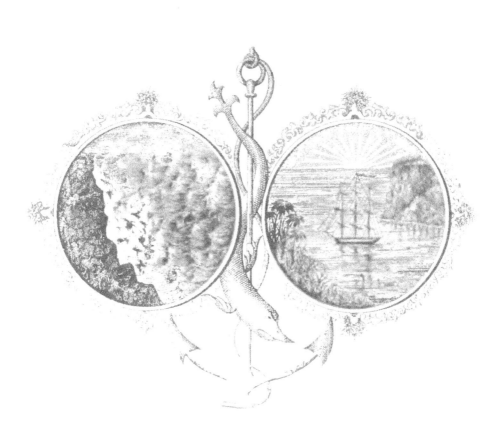

Hark! Hear you complainings? Dry leaves find
    a voice!
  Through the storm their complainings I hear:
" Storm, drive us not so in your wrath." But no
    choice!
Does the storm care for leaves old and sere?
  Moaning, groaning dead leaves do I hear.

Old age! Still clinging to life—sere and old—
  Like Autumn brown leaf to its tree.
What wonder with death-grip to Earth he doth
    hold—
That he fears the dark launching away?
  Swinging, clinging to Time and to Day?

Stormy death-night is falling—how dark and how
    chill!
  See! the sere leaf is trembling o'erhead.
How long, aged sinner, canst cling up there still?

How far to the Land of the Dead?

    Swinging, clinging—poor soul—overhead.

A hurricane sweepeth - God's tempests awake;

    Like chaff which the winds drive away,

Brown leaves—sere souls—shaken loose do they

    take

And sweep from the earth far away—

    Fearing, nearing Eternity's Day.

Are storms wrong in driving dead leaves from

    the tree?

    Or God, to drive sinners away?

Yet who can but weep such a sad loss to see?

Oh! what must the soul feel, I pray—

    Shaken, taken by God's wrath away?

Oh! such a sad funeral—such hopeless grave!

    Hear the bells of Eternity toll!

Even Angels might weep—yet no pity can save.

Oh! what must this mean: *A Lost Soul!*

    Sad bells of Eternity, toll!

II.

Ripe fruits are hanging on vine and on tree;

    Golden apples and grapes, rich and rare.

The Autumn hath borne a choice harvest for thee,

And a vintage surpassingly fair:

    Ripened, golden, for husbandman's care.

Stormy Winter is coming o'er orchard and wold,

    But the fruit by the kindliest hand,

Is garnered and safe from the winds and the cold:

In the storms the bare trees alone stand.

    Fruit is garnered by husbandman's hand.

Human souls have been nearing the harvest

    time—

Have ripened through night and through day;
Are ready for garner by Hand Divine—
To be plucked—to be stored away
    In the Garners of Upper Day !

Not driven like leaves sere and dead from the
        tree ;
    But touched by the finger of Love,
And carried away to Eternity—
From the Earth to the Land above,
    By the hand of Eternal Love!

See ! Ships are there nearing the Quiet Bay ;
    And the land is in sight just before ;
And out from the Dark they are sailing to Day ;
In from sea, they cast anchor at shore—
    Drifting, tossing on ocean no more!

The Harbor's smooth waters are clear as the
        glass.

Inexpressibly sweet there to be

All quiet and safe when the rough sea we pass;

From the storms and the wreck-dangers free—

In the Harbor at last from the Sea!

Sails were torn, masts broken, and well nigh were

lost

In the waves, all the Ships in the Bay:—

Over treacherous shoals—by the wild winds were

tossed,

And driven far out of their way—

These Ships, anchored safe in the Bay!

So souls from the Earth are there nearing the

Land.

And Eternity lies just before!

From seas they come in—they are touching the

strand :

Casting anchor at last by the shore—

3

Drifting, tossing on ocean no more.

O thou Harbor of God smooth and clear as the
glass!
Inexpressibly sweet here to rest
All quiet and safe on thy bosom! We pass
From the seas to the Land of the Blest.
Inexpressibly sweet here to rest!

Fears sickened and tossed these same souls many
days;
They were driven by winds, and were tossed!
O'er the seas, in the dark, how devious their
ways;—
Over shoals, mid the storms—nearly lost;
Fearful, drifting, driven, shattered and tossed!

From rough, stormy Ocean, to calm Heavenly
Strand;
From sea-dangers, to well-guarded Bay;

From the rocks and the surf, cast we anchor at
    Land ;
From the night, glide our ships to the day.
    Step we off on the Shore Far Away!

"MIGHTY TO SAVE."

HEB. VII: 25.

The Sea's deep world of waters—
Oh! can it not uphold a boat,
And keep its infant weight afloat?
Doth Ocean faint or weary grow?
Do Ocean tides cease ebb and flow
For skiff upon its waves afloat?

The Sea's deep, mighty waters
Can, with like ease, uplift and bear
The mightiest ship given to its care!
No weight of heaviest, longest keel
Can make the Ocean ever feel
A burden hard for waves to bear!

The Sea's deep world of waters,

Like giant arms round infant form,

Floats easy through the calm and storm

The fragile skiff, or fisher's boat,

And keeps man's proudest ships afloat.

Nothing can weary or alarm !

Souls have a Mighty Savior !

Can Jesus not uplift our care ?

Can Jesus not our burdens bear ?

And is there, then, some heaviest grief

For which He cannot find relief ?

Some burden Jesus cannot bear ?

Souls have a Mighty Savior !

Our smallest grief, as fragile boat

Upon the Ocean's waves afloat—

Our heaviest hours of wild unrest,

Like great ships on the Ocean's breast,

With equal ease He keeps afloat.

Souls have a Mighty Savior !
Able, when willing ; willing, when
He hears the soul's quick cry of pain.
Christ's garment-hem flows mid the throngs ;
A touch is cure for human wrongs.
His garment-hem heals human pain.

Souls have a Mighty Savior !
And but to hear Him " passing by,"
When needy souls to Jesus cry,
Blind eyes are opened to the day ;
Night—human sorrow—fades away ;
Souls gaze upon new earth and sky.

Souls have a Mighty Savior !
With hands fast nailed to accursed Tree,
A thief-cry falls : " Remember me."
Snatched from the jaws of Death and Hell,

Through all Eternity he 'll tell
How great a Savior Christ can be.

Souls have a Mighty Savior!
Cast all thy burdens on the Lord;
Beneath thee is His sacred Word.
No storm can drift thee far from shore;
Fear not Life's angriest ocean-roar;
Himself each angry wind hath stirred!

Trust to thy Mighty Savior!
On Galilee He sails to-day;
For thee He 'll quickly rise and say :
" Be still." How soon will hush to rest
Each passion of the human breast!
How great the calm! How smooth the Sea!

THE HIGHER WAY.

ISA. LV. 9.

Is it darkness, Earth, for thee?
Through the shadows and the vapors,
Fragrant flowers become wierd tapers
Raising sad thoughts, starting tears!
Yet be glad, O Earth for shadows;
Flowers and meadows
Need the night as well as day.
What seems weary wild, and dreary
Desert where all joys delay,
When the Night strikes tent inglorious,
All victorious
Light encamps! Night blesses day!

Is it night time, Soul, for thee?

From the surges, loudest dashing,

Glinteth, brightest silver flashing

On Life's rainy, stormy sea.

Out from darkness cometh brightness!

                   If not sightless,

Soul, thou'lt see the dawning soon.

For, forever, soul endeavor

Turns noon-night to day-time noon.

Brightest hopes, O soul, far scattered,

                     Tempest shattered,

God can save!   Night turns to noon!

        Night and storms are best for thee.

Clouds are blessings—drifting—drifting;

Shadows shifting, drifting, shifting!

Too much sun and too much day

Wither flowers and wolds and meadows!—

              Best that shadows

Come between the sun and thee.

On Life's Ocean, no commotion

Dangerous as calm can be!

Sluggish waves—toil unavailing—

                There's no sailing!

Best are night and storms for thee!

         God doth send what's best for thee.

Diamonds shine by grinding roughest.

Winds make oak trees grow the toughest.

Rainy, sodden days are blest.

O my soul, oft sad and weary,

                Grow more cheery;

This is God's hand feeding thee.

No land scourges—no sea surges

Can do harm, or victors be!

Sweetest things are fed by raining:

                Storms are training

Souls for blest Eternity!

LONGING AND SATISFIED.

No weary seaman more desires the land—

The dear Home-Land—

Whose heart hath waited long and yearned to be

With those he loved beyond the dangerous sea,

Than do I yearn

Homeward my face to turn,

And be with Thee.

No poor lost wanderer through the stormy night—

The starless night—

Watches first streakings of the dawn to see,

More than my heart, where Thou art, longs to be—

Than I desire

To hear Thee: " Come up higher "—

" Come unto Me ! "

Lord, I have struggled through the by-gone
    years—

The weary years—

To find sweet rest ; where like a weary bird

My soul might fold her wings—no storm-wind
    heard !—

Where peace and rest,

And not this weariness,

Might fall on me.

So, with each day, through storms or sunny sky—

Bright or dark sky—

I 've hoped and prayed through many blinding
    tears

To find Thy face along the earthly years ;—

That peace and love

Would come from God above

And· dwell with me!

And when the night came down in silence deep,

Bringing its sleep,

On bended knees in loneliest places, there

My soul hath wearied Heaven with pleading

prayer

That I might be

Led—ever led by Thee

The way to see!

Why must it be no seaman longs for land—

The dear Home-Land—

As still my heart doth go—doth ever go

Through heights above —through untold depths

below,

Longing for love—

For only Thy dear love

     And Home above?

Oh! shall I e'er upon some shoreward wave

     Some homeward wave—

Drift in at last to Harbor—wanderings o'er?

O soul of mine, shall you and I reach shore?—

     Drift in at last

Where anchor may be cast—

     These storms all past?

SATISFIED.

As weary seaman greets once more the land—

     The dear Home-Land—And

leaves behind the treacherous, stormy main, And

gains sweet rest, and lays aside all pain—

     So, satisfied,

Upon this shore-ward tide

    I come to Thee!

As poor lost wanderer from the stormy night—

    The starless night—

Gladly the outlines of the Morn doth see,

Watcheth the joy come and the sorrow flee—

    So here at last,

With storms all drifted past,

    I come to Thee!

How bright will be the eternal, changeless

    years—

    Heaven's nightless years!

Here find I rest! Just like some weary bird

My soul doth fold her wings — no storm-wind

    heard.

    Nor wind, nor wave

On Galilee doth rave—

    Rebuked by Thee!

Here press my feet the furthest outward shore—
        Life's margin shore !
Looking across, I so desire to go !
I long to leave this side—to see—to know
        That other shore
Far off—" The Evermore "—
        And be with Thee.

Ah ! well, at last upon this shoreward wave—
        This Homeward wave—
I've drifted into Harbor—dangers o'er.
I've ceased to wander—now adrift no more,
        The Sea is past ;—
My anchor drops at last—
        The storms all past.

Soul, thou art satisfied.   God gives thee rest—
        Such happy rest !
The Gate all Beautiful swings open wide ;

I enter in upon this Heavenly tide.

How blest to see

The King, eternally!

In Heaven to be!

THE LOST SHEEP.

Far—far on mountains cold, in want and danger,
　　　　The Lost is wandering.
To all around a lonely foldless stranger—
　　　　A needy, bleating thing.

Far—far from pastures green hath it been straying,
　　　　From waters cold and still :
In rains and storms long, late hath it been staying—
　　　　Like one of perverse will!

The snow, and ice, and mountain barrennesses
　　　　Are not like pastures fair ;
The want, and dangers, and the deep distresses—
　　　　Not these the sheep-fold share.

How shall the lost return?   Night's darkest
    shadows
            Shut out the sheep-track way !
The path is lost back to the shades and meadows
            From whence his feet did stray.

And angry voices howl around the stranger,
            And death-falls everywhere.
The Lost One dwells amid the deepest danger
            On mountains of despair !

Is that a soul on Sin's dark mountains straying—
            Like Lost Sheep from its fold ?
From God's safe pasturage long—late delaying—
            Needy, and lost, and cold ?

Far—far away, almost beyond God's calling,
            O human soul, stand still.
Shadows of death around thy way are falling,
            Dangers thy pathway fill !

Swamps, moorlands, pitfalls, angry beasts of
   preying,
       Hedge up thy backward way;
O soul, why—whither art thou blindly straying
       Mid night and dangers, say?

Good Shepherd, with thy tender heart all loving—
       Seeking the Lost Ones here,
O see my soul on barren mountains roving,
       And save me from despair!

Thy weary foot-marks, stained with blood are
   going—
       Journeying at priceless cost :
Thy tenderest love on thankless souls bestowing,
       Seeking to save the Lost!

Long—long the road! As far as Earth from
   Heaven!
       Dark—dark and cruel road!

To seek and save — how much the Shepherd's
    given
        To lead us back to God.

His love hath borne thee, soul of mine, from
    danger,
        In from the night and cold.
No more on mountains bleak art thou a stranger,
        But safe in Jesus' Fold.

And home-like, good, and tender is the hiding
        He gives thee from all harm
Green pastures, living waters, and no chiding
        Within His Sheep-Fold warm.

Not now on dreary wastes, with stranger sad-
    ness ;—
        No unknown, sin-filled hills !
Within His Pastures all is sweet home gladness
        Beside fair Heavenly rills.

RELEASE.

I.

In Jerusalem the olden
    The Lord's Disciple lay,
By inner dungeon holden
    From light of God's bright day,
Dreaming of the Golden
    Jerusalem far away!

An Angel from far Glory—
    From Courts of Endless Day,
Sped to the prison hoary
    Where God's Disciple lay:

Told him the wondrous story
    And led him out to day.

Out in the city olden!
    Free from the prison walls!
By no dark dungeon holden—
    Where quiet starlight falls!—
Prophet of City Golden
    With Jasper Gates and Walls!

Behind him dungeon dreary,
    With bolts and iron bars,
And days and nights all weary—
    Above him, throbbing stars!
He hears with spirit cheery
    The Gate's harsh grating bars!

II.

A soul in city olden,
    Ready to pass away,

By pains and anguish holden,
　　Upon his pallet lay,
Dreaming of the Golden
　　Jerusalem far away.

Death-Angel from far Glory
　　Sped, touched Him where he lay
Within his prison hoary,
　　And led him out to day—
Sped up the Hills of Glory
　　Where Town Celestial lay!

Light from its Walls was streaming—
　　Sounds from its River sang—
Joy from its Gates was gleaming—
　　Praise from its Towers rang!—
On earth, like noise in dreaming,
　　The Iron Gate's harsh clang!

Weeping, and bells slow-ringing,

Far—far away below !

Here sweetest choirs are singing ;

Here softest rivers flow ;

Here Heaven's streets are ringing ;

Here Angel armies go !

How softly down there closes

The gates of Human Life !

How calm the soul reposes

After its bitter strife !

How soundless his hand closes

The Iron Gates of Life !

THE DOOR.

JOHN X:7.

"I am the only Door :
Through me ye enter on the Eternal Years :
I shut without all earthly woes and fears :
All Sin's dark sorrows, and Care's pressing crowd :
And passions, jostling, swaying, shouting loud!
I am the only Door!"

I stand before this Door.
Around me crowd my untold dreary days.
I think it strange my longing heart delays
To press within the open Door, and be
From all this throng forever far and free
Inside the open Door!

Outside the open Door :—

Amid the joys and hopes, like dreams, ideal,

Missing the soul's fruition, rich and real :

A blind star-gazer, spending Life star-gazing :

A dumb earth-praiser, spending Life earth-

praising

'Outside the open Door !

" Come soul, I am the Door ! "

No silvery bell hath ever sweeter chime

Adown the echoing corridors of Time,

Than this sweet voice which bids me enter in

And all the treasures of my longing win

Within this open Door.

I linger at the Door.

A thousand echoes from behind me ring

From out the Past—and countless memories sting

Within my soul : yet here I lingering stay :

And His sweet voice in sweetest tones doth say :
  "Come soul, I am the Door—

  " I am the only Door !
A Mansion in the eternal years for thee
Is ready waiting, if thou comest to Me :
And by the River which hath crystal flow
Thy ransomed soul in sweetest rest shall go
  Through this wide open door.

  " Faith entereth the Door.
Faith seizeth on the Kingdom—walketh free
And joineth in Heaven's wondrous melody,
And saileth on the windless Ocean there
Before the Throne, all glorious and fair!
  Faith's key unlocks the Door !"

  O Christ, the sinner's Door,
A sinful soul, by Faith, I come to thee.

Weary, and late, and longing, pity me.

And as I cross Thy threshold, wondrous, o'er,

Come o'er the threshold of my lowly door,

And leave me nevermore!

FRUITLESS TOIL.

All night they toiled on Galilee;
Weary and hard till dawn of day.

Their empty nets no fishes took;
'T was fruitless toil, 't was thankless work.

But at the dawning of the day,
A stranger stood by Galilee.

" Cast to the right thy net."   They cast,
And found abundant fish at last.

Instead of fruitless toil, and night;
It is success, and morning light.

We toil like they of Galilee :
Weary and useless toil as they.

We yearn for fish within our net.
We drag, and find no fishes yet!

Our hearts seek something ; and we be
Like fruitless toilers on the sea.

Wet nets, and heavy ; weary hands ;
Much toil and many heart-demands !

We see so little good we gain ;
We miss the fruit, and keep the pain.

What's wrong ?   Why fruitless energy ?
What's wrong ?   We toil enough and try !

We need that Voice to guide us, too—
Our way to lead—our duty, show.

There's water—so we drop our net.

'T is not right place: no fish we get.

There's work undone you try to do :

You fail.   That work was not for you :—

Some friend to save ! Why wandering still?

Your word was wrong, though right your will.

Ne'er up to God will float the song

In notes all right from heart all wrong!

Far better is it to our God

From humblest heart to hear right word,

Than loftiest strains of rapturous song

From souls that sing God's glory wrong!

Without the Master's Voice to guide,

We miss the pathway o'er the tide.

And all night long on Galilee
We fruitless toil till break of day!

O Jesus, Master, come to me,
A weary toiler on the sea!

Let day-break dawn upon my heart,
And let thy voice new hope impart,

And tell me where my net to cast
That work may have reward at last!

"TOWARD THE MARK."

PHIL. III: 14.

This is the day-time, given to thee
To work and fight in faithfully.
No earnest toil will be in vain;
'Twill bud, and bloom, and fruit again.

This is the sharp campaigning hour!
Needed: mind strength, heart nerve, soul power!
No march that leads not faithful feet
Nearer the Camp within the Gate.

This is the sultry time of noon;
The heat and dust must now be borne.
No sweat-drops here are useless there;
No burdens given too great to bear.

The day-time! Night soon cometh on.
The sharp campaigning will be done!
No work at night; and camping place
Is not where winners run the race!

Often we read not things aright.
Amid the work—amid the fight,
Borne down with burdens, dimmed with smoke,
The fight seems lost, and sore the yoke.

Sharp fight with human doubts and sin,
With foes without and foes within,
Availeth much to lift the soul
Up to the Life's supremest goal.

What if, at times, our hopes are vain?
Our fears are foes! They but enchain
And fetter us! True souls and brave
Will drive the foe and victory have!

As not alone o'er Eastern skies
The quiet day-dawn softly lies,
But far away o'er hill tops bright,
Behind us bathes the world in light;

So faithfulness in deed or word
Is in no one spot seen or heard;
But far away it molds, and lives,
And new impulse to faint heart gives.

This is a world where all we do
Is ever living, ever new.
Good deeds encamp on Heavenly Plains,
As mountain streams find out the main.

Courage my brother! Endless gain
Follows upon the fleeting pain!
The camping ground will end the fight,
And bright day follows on the night;

Eternal gain for temporal loss ;

And Heavenly Crown for Earthly Cross!

For bondage here, there's sure release ;

For tossings now, then blessed peace.

For service here in Christ's name given,

Up there for thee, a Home in Heaven!

Who sees before him and would be

A laggard toward Eternity?

The sun shines hot!   'Tis sultry noon!

Press forward!   Evening cometh soon!

FAR BETTER.

PHIL. 1:23.

I stayed in a fisherman's hut
Beside the stormy sea—
The wind-driven, stormy sea!
      The sands gave way.
      One stormy day,
And slid my hut from me away.
But was that loss to me?

I live in a Palace Home
Where there is "no more sea"—
No wind-driven, stormy sea!
      Foundations sure
      That shall endure—
Eternal Rock beneath me, sure!
"Far better" here to be.

I stayed in a pilgrim tent,
Pitched in a barren land—
A thirsty, barren land!
       The winds did lift
       My tent and drift
It far away!   The winds did lift
My tent from out my hand!

'Tis a stately mansion here
In a fruitful, plenteous Land—
A safe and goodly Land.
       No winds do blow
       To overthrow
My home up here, as down below.
" Far better " is this Land.

I was banished, lonely, sad ;
An exile forced to be
From one most dear to me !

, Dark moorlands lay
Athwart my way.
And such dark night shut out my day.
At home I could not be.

I am home, joyous, glad!
And Christ's dear face I see—
With Him eternally!
The earth hath joy,
But much alloy;
And many fears and sins annoy.
" Far better " here to be
Safe home eternally!

WISDOM.

JOB XXVIII.

One question through the thousand years
Breaks on the millions' listening ears ;
Asked oftentime in gloom and fears.

Asked of the Depth : " 'Tis not in me ! "
Asked of the ever throbbing Sea :
" Nor can it in my caverns be ! "

Can it be gotten with fine gold ?
Hath silver weight its value told ?
Can it for jewels fine be sold ?

Is Wisdom weighed for Pearls, or ore
Floated from far-famed Ophir's shore ?
Rubies or Emeralds bring it o'er ?

Hid close from every bird of air—
Destruction stands with curious stare—
And Death cries: "Wisdom is not here!"

The Great Almighty God hath spoken;
From out the skies He gives us token:
Silence of centuries is broken!

For what can hide from His great eye
Who sweepeth through remotest sky,
And sees where all things hidden lie?

Who cutteth channels for each river?
Who swingeth worlds onward forever?
Of might and good, the only giver?

Who stretcheth out His tent-like sky—
Who hangs out world on world on high,
And, unperceived, swift passeth by?

Who forms the treasures of the snow—
Who binds the earth-streams overflow—
Who makes the oceans ebb and flow?

Who shakes the hoar-frost from His hand—
Who rides sublime o'er every land—
Whose deep ways none can understand?

Oh! what can hide from Him, or be
A secret to the All-seeing Eye,
In air or ocean? Earth or sky?

He knows where truest Wisdom lies!
His warning drops from far-off skies.
Hearken and be thou truly wise:

"Fear God with godly fear. Depart
From evil with a humble heart;
And Wisdom gain—Life's truest part."

The question 's answered which the Years
Have asked with many anxious tears—
Still stumbling on through doubts and fears!

The riddles of the earth are read :
Life waves pour not in Sea called " Dead ;"
They break on far-off shores instead!

Sun after sun goes down the skies,
Wave after wave swells, ebbs and dies,
Death breaks on life beyond the skies!

When doubts sweep in embattled line
Across the soul, this clear sunshine
Shall melt their ranks by warmth Divine.

When earthly foes of every form
Press on the soul, swarm after swarm,
This Voice rides down each angry storm!

For what men guessed, we surely know :

Each life-wave hath eternal flow,

And Spring doth burst from ice and snow.

Divinest Wisdom this : To fear

Our God, and turn from evil here,

And meet His great " Well-done " up there.

ADRIFT.

Like some great ship befogged at sea,
No land-marks out, no star-marks given,
The human soul that breaks control
And from the old, old Faith is driven.

Far will it voyage seeking rest ;
And hearken with suspended oar ;
Will drift—will row—ever in quest
Of sights along some well-known shore ;

Will seek in vain to catch the sound
Of the low rote of waters clear
That break along the Heavenly Strand,
Which Faith can see, and bring so near.

Fog bells may ring, but never comes
An answering echo.   All is doubt!
No clear blue skies—no well-known hills !
All lights in heaven and earth are out.

In vain for human soul, alone,
Faithless, to try Life's unknown sea.
Contrary winds, cross currents, storms
Will drive it ever hopelessly.

One cannot find the Steadfast Hills
And glorious Plains of Paradise;
One ne'er shall hear the Living Rills,
And see the Pearly Walls arise ;

One ne'er shall view with vision clear
The sea paths over Life's vast tide ;
Never shall find sweet comfort here ;
Nor ever in God's Harbor ride ;

Who lays his own hand on the helm,
Or pulls with human might the oar!—
Who steers not by the North Star given,
But follows false lights on the shore !

But what if, when quick storms arise
And sweep the soul's night Galilee,
Uprolling waves and darkening skies,
The Christ were sailing there with thee ?

What if, amid our doubts and pains,
Struggling with adverse winds and sea,
Walking along the watery plains,
That Form Divine should come to thee ?

The noisy seas would hush : the storm
Of doubts grow calm at His great will :
Contrary winds would cease to harm :
And every throbbing wave be still.

Then, Hills of Paradise would lift
Their virid sheen beyond the tide.
For souls which take·Faith's Christ on board
Shall every stormy sea outride.

For Faith shall touch the longed for shore ;
Its anchor drop within the veil
Where adverse storms will all be o'er,
And never wind or wave assail!

O toilers on Doubt's dreary sea,
Where stars are out and storms sweep sore,
The Lord Christ cometh close to thee—
Nearer, because you need Him more.

For need of Christ is cry to Him ;
And, never absent very far,
When rowing mid the shadows dim,
He 's closest where the neediest are.

Take Christ on board. Faith conquers Doubt!

Let Him stand at the helm for thee,

And soon thy Bark will touch the Land Where

there is no more stormy sea!

WORK.

ECCLES. IX: 10.

Harvest is ripe to-day.

Fields are all white and ready.

Sheaves for the reaper's pay—

For willing hands and steady!

Thrust in thy sickle keen ;

Gather the golden grain.

To-morrow no ripe harvest leaves.

        Only "a little while"

To bind the golden sheaves !

Harvest is ripe to-day.

Rich grain for true endeavor !

Fritter the hours away,

You lose reward forever.

Thrust in! Work earnestly!

Harvest is but a day.

Dust—noon-day heat and rapid labor—

Only "a little while!"

Harvest repays endeavor!

Life Gates swing wide to-day,

Inviting soul-endeavor.

My soul, thy God doth say:

"Enter; 'tis now, or never!

Go! toil, speak, act, and pray;

Life is a swift sharp day;

Life has no morrow, soul, for thee.

Only 'a little while'

To make Eternity!"

Lift up thine eyes to-day.

Fields are all white for reaping.

They will not brook delay ;
Life is too brief for sleeping.
Thrust in thy sickle keen !
Bind, gather, garner, glean !
Harvest is mighty—reapers, few.
       Only "a little while"
To do what thou canst do !

Life surges rise to-day,
The tide is outward swelling.
Soul, quick ! push off ! away !
This strand holds not thy dwelling.
At flood-tide haste to sea !
Weigh anchor—ready be !
Life's ebbing waves wait not for man.
       Only "a little while—"
Improve it as you can.

Over Life's skies to-day

The clouds go drifting—drifting ;

Their shadows cross the way

With ever restless shifting.

Currents of tireless care

Assail me everywhere.

God's hand can sweep all clouds away.

        Only " a little while "

From darkness into day.

Be strong—be true, to-day.

A little while of drifting

O'er rocky, watery way—

A little restless shifting—

A little while of sorrow—

Then breaks the glad to-morrow !

God will cast anchor then for thee.

        Only a "little while ; "

Time meets Eternity.

NEW HOME.

Oh! wondrous fair
Hath this life grown to me at last!
I love to think that all is past
  That was so weary there!

  'Twas wondrous grace!
God took me from the depth and gloom;
He swept and garnished my soul room,
  And made it a new place.

  A Cottage low:
'Tis true my life 's no Palace Home;
No lofty walls—no bending dome—
  Only a Cottage low.

But life can be

Most happy in a Cottage spent,

With heart and hand on duty bent,

    And purpose to please Thee.

Abide, dear Lord,

Within my Cottage walls.   O come

And bless me in my lowly home!

    And help me on my road!

Jesus, so kind!

Our Cottage Walls may hear thy voice ;

And humblest hearts are Thy sweet choice—

    On earth Thy rest to find!

In Bethany

On quiet slope of Olivet

The lowly home Thy presence met—

    Oh! come and sup with me!

And well I know

When winds lift off this earthly tent,

And Death's rude hand its seams has rent—

The inmate then shall go

To dwell above

In stately Mansion built all fair,

Beyond Life's din and fever jar,

And lit with Jesus' love !

THE CAMP.

I.

On the billowy sands
    In the age Long-Ago
A strange Pillar stands
    O'er the tents lying low.
Cloud Pillar by day,
    Light Pillar by night;
A Guide for the way
    And a Shield for the right.

When the gloom of the night
    Fills the Desert's lone camps,
The tent-homes are bright

From the low-swinging lamps.
Like sheep in the fold
    Sheltered safely from fear,
The white flock of old
    Hath the Good Shepherd near.

'Tis the Camp of the Lord.
    The frail tents on the sand
Have beneath them His Word
    And His Almighty Hand!
No brood is so safe
    Neath the feathery wing,
As souls on the waste
    Which to God closely cling!

From Goshen they came;
    And the Sea Door swung wide,
And the Pillar of Flame
    Led them safe to this side.

Past Marah's marsh pool,

  Past Elim's soft palms,

They are marching with God

  Through the storms and the calms.

II.

O'er the Campment of Souls

  The tall Pillar of God

Leads on the great march

  Which the " worthies have trod."

Cloud Pillar by day,

  Fire Pillar by night;

A Guide for the way

  And a Guard for the right.

When the gloom of Distress

  Fills the Desert's lone Camp,

Light falleth to bless

From God's bright swinging Lamp.
And the billowy waste
Greets the River's fair flow
Which is cool to the taste
Of the Pilgrims below.

If Marah's brack lake
We faint at to-day,
Soon Elim will break
On our eyes by the way ;
And each shadowy palm,
And each deep living well,
With their green cooling calm
The Fair Canaan fortell.

O the Camp of the Lord !
From Egypt we came.
And we follow his Word
And His Pillar of Flame.

Red Seas cannot stay
>   The march of the soul
On its Wilderness Way
>   To the Heavenly Goal.

When the sands lie behind
>   And Canaan is near,
What joy shall we find,
>   And what absence of fear!
On Jericho's Plain
>   The fair City of Green
Shall banish all pain
>   With its bright golden sheen.

And the army shall stand
>   Neath the feathery palms
In the Glorious Land
>   Mid the Heavenly Calms.
And the Desert will lie

Far away—long ago
From the City on high·
Where the Sanctified go.

"THE FIELD IS THE WORLD."

MATT. XIII: 38.

"The field is this great world:—

                  But, Lord, how bare—

How treeless, grassless, dewless, seems the field!

How parched its plains beneath the sun's fierce

    stare ;

And for one's labor scanty harvests yield!

"The field is this great world:—"

                But, Lord, how long

It takes the seed upon such field to grow!

The reaper, waiting, gives up cheer and song—

And even seedsman scarce finds heart to sow!

" The field is this great world :—"

But, Lord, how deep
The night to eyes that watch for harvest morn !
And tares are sown if weary watchers sleep—
And thistles wave among the ripening corn !

But weary reaper, watch, and work, and wait :
The sailor watcheth mid the angry roar
Of waters on the reef-bound shore that break ;—
Watcheth and waiteth till the storm is o'er.

O reaper, wait ! The absent Husbandman
Will come full quickly as He said to thee.
And resting comes where weary waitings end ;
And full ripe sheaves the sure reward shall be !

O reaper, work ! Are fields all drained of dew ?
Is earth all parched—trees bare—and grass blades
    dry ?

The fields are green—the fruitage ever new—
The Land is fair beyond the sunset sky.

My soul, grow strong to watch, and work, and
    wait!
Sight follows Faith.   No part of life is vain.
What's done, or borne, upon thy Lord's Estate
Grows to rich harvest on the Heavenly Plain.

The weary night-watch where the breakers roar—
The patient waiting where no signs are seen—
The work on sunbrowned fields or dewless shore
Shall wave at last Eternal Fields of Green!

MARAH AND ELIM.

I sat by Marah's brackish pool
My burning thirst to slake and cool.

Through weary days in stranger land
My feet had parched along the sand.

When tongue is dry and lips are hot
How strange God leads to such a spot:—

To lead one here to Marah's pool
With bitter waters thirst to cool !

God leads to bitter lake the feet
That Elim Wells may taste more sweet.

Cooler and greener for the hot
Dry bitter sands at Marah's spot.

Earth is the Marah! Pilgrims drink
Oft at the bitter, brackish brink.

Yet here we stay not—pitch no tent.
Sorrows are transient—only lent.

Red Seas and Marahs mark the way
To Elim's soft and cooling stay.

Oh! how *His* bitter pangs I prize,
When from some Marah my wet eyes

Fall on that Cross where *He* did drink
The bitterest draughts at Marah's brink!

Read clearly that God's hand doth send
Bitter and sweet for some wise end.

Heirs! When a little older grown,
Ours is the Crown and glorious Throne.

Exiles! Just round that Headland lies
The Homelike Hills of Paradise.

Children! On Desert sands we roam
Where all the paths are leading Home.

Sand all around! Marah is here!
Lift up thine eyes—Elim is near!

Faith sees its Fountains, greets its Palms,
Is mustered out in Heavenly Lands,
And pitches tent amid their Calms!

MASTER MUSICIAN.

An instrument with noiseless strings
And soundless chords, unstrung and still,
Waited for Master Hand that brings
Divinest music where He will.

The Leader of the Choir above
Came to my heart unstrung and still.
He touched the key-note He called: "Love,"
And struck it with Omniscient skill!

And now a new song I can sing—
My heart the music sweet affords;

And all my powers with joy-thrills ring
The echoes of the Love-trilled chords!

And should my heart discordant sound,
The Master tuneth fresh its keys
Until through all its strings resound
The wondrous Love-touched harmonies.

O Master Leader of the Choir
Which sings Eternal Love on high,
When out of tune, my heart inspire—
When harsh or soundless, be Thou nigh.

For hearts of men should echo God!
For hearts of men should sing His Love!
For hearts of men on Pilgrim road
Should join the strains of Choirs above!

PROVIDENCE.

MATT. VI. 26, 28, 30.

Up and down with cheerless cry
Dusky wings beat through the sky ;
And God hears the raven's cry.

  Doth His care reach silly things
  Beating on their weary wings?
  Doth God feed such witless things?
  Care for birds that fill the sky ?

Will he not hear souls that cry?

On the pine tree's swaying crest
Sparrows hang their fragile nest ;
And our God doth give them rest.

Humble sparrows God doth see

Swinging on each lonely tree;

When one falleth God doth see.

O my soul, why dost thou fear?

Will not God thy cravings hear?

How the lilies mid the cold,

On the hill-slopes, in the wold,

God doth clothe fold upon fold:

Weaves them beauteous garments where

Chilly blast and sea-side air

Bend the lilies, God's sweet care!

Doth God clothe field-lilies? He

Will much more, my soul, clothe thee!

Not a raven's cheerless cry—

Not a wing-beat on the sky,

God's quick ear e'er passeth by!

Not a sparrow's wind-swung nest;

Not a lily's mute request,

But there falls our God's kind rest.

O my doubting soul, will He

Not much more thy refuge be?

PRECIOUS SEED.

PSALM CXXVI: 6.

I.

What are you scattering, husbandman?
Wheat, bringing goodly sheaves at last?
Is that not only chaff you cast

       Upon your fields—
       Broad fertile fields?

And will your chaff to harvest grow—
Ripe, waving fields of grain e'èr show?
Why scatter chaff, O husbandman?

What are you planting, husbandman?
Only a thorn?   Why toil you so?

Do figs from thorns and brambles grow?—

    Grapes, ripe and fair,

    Shall men pluck there?

Grapes grown from thorns? Joy plucked from

  Pain?

Why plant, and toil, and hope in vain?

What are you planting, husbandman?

The same hard toiling, husbandman,

It takes thee thy poor chaff to sow—

Hard labor only briers to grow!

    Plant vines instead;—

    And wheat for bread.

Shrub oaks demand same care and pain

As cedars fair of Lebanon!

Why plant shrub oaks then, husbandman?

II

What sowest thou, soul husbandman?
This Life hath many " precious seed "
To sow against the time of need.
                    Yet God doth know
                    We often sow
Our worldly thistles on the wind,
And wonder we no harvest find !
What sowest thou, soul husbandman?

What art thou planting, husbandman?
Kind words and loving deeds will grow
To goodly trees whose branches throw
                    Fair grateful shades
                    O'er weary heads;
'Their leaves for healing human hearts
Of many cares and bitter smarts.
Plant Christ-like deeds, O husbandman !

And scatter broad-cast, husbandman ;
And by all waters !   God will see
That Harvest-time shall come to thee.
    Nor canst thou know
    Which seed will grow—
The early or the later sown ;
But God thy labors all will own.
Stay not thy hand, soul husbandman !

If one could know, O husbandman,
What hearts are filled, what souls made glad
By our Life-sowing, often sad—
    If, through our tears,
    Our doubts and fears,
We could but see the hungry fed,
And, by our words, the erring led,
Would we then weary, husbandman ?

If we could know, O husbandman,

The harvest of the Upper Day,
Grown from the seed by Life's hard way—
   If we could see
   Eternity,
While planting, sowing here, who then
Would scatter thorns and briars again?
We would sow well, O husbandman!

Work, you and I, soul husbandman!
God's eye doth mark each " precious seed ;"
His rains, dews, light and air will feed.
   From winter's snow
   And storms below,
The seed will burst—rich Harvest be
On Heavenly Plains for you and me!
Bear " precious seed," soul husbandman.

DAILY BREAD

MATT. VI: II.

The sandaled hosts of Israel trod
The Wilderness, led by their God.

And night by night the Manna fell
To feed the hosts of Israel.

Around their white tents, like the dew
It lay each morning, fresh and new.

Enough for all—a bounteous store
Of daily bread! Enough—no more.

"Give us this day our daily bread."
How many millions God hath fed.

8

When nights of want and sorrow rise,
God's Manna drops from far off skies.

Soul food, like hoar-frost on the hills,
For daily need His love distils.

The sandaled pilgrims of the Lord
Waiting, still feed upon His word.

O'er all the sands of Life still lies
The Manna dropped from far off skies.

Around our pilgrim tents the store
Is full for daily wants:—no more!

Like dews on Hermon's hills, each day
Distils Thy love along Life's way.

And never cry is made for bread
When stone is given to hearts instead.

For each new sorrow, fresh new balm ;
For each new strife, God-given calm.

For daily cares new strength is given
Till earthly waves shall strike on Heaven !

Earth pilgrims, we ; with sandaled feet
Tenting below without the Gate.

Each night the rearguard, weary, sore,
Is where the vanguard was before.

And Manna falls along the way—
Our daily bread for each new day.

O human souls, contented be.
God gives enough to you and me ;

Till pilgrim souls shall reach the River
Cleaving the Now from the Forever!

Old corn of Canaan will be given—

And fruits Divine to souls in Heaven.

"IT WINNA FASH ME LANG.'

It winna fash me lang
That life was dark and dreary.
It canna brak the Heavenly sang
That mony days war weary.
And, runnin' doun the last steep hill.
This pack o' waes will soon be still.

I dinna min' the stane
My weary fit hae stricken.
I stumble towards my langed for Hame—
But, whyles, my heart will sicken.
It winna matter : God's guid way
Rins through the shadows up to day.

Nae anguish and nae scorn—

Hame-sickness and nae sadness—

Nae Roman spear—nae Pilate's thorn—

Nae mob's wild cry o' madness

Sae heavy fa's on you an' me

As on the Christ o' Calvary!

I need na bear it lang—

Nae pilgrim cross forever!

The gowden crown, the thrilling sang

Are just beyond the River.

Ane need na dread the Harbor Bar

Wha lang hae sailed owre seas afar!

O Gowden Gates on high!

O harps and choirs immortal!

My soul wad climb the loftiest sky

And pass the Pearly Portal!

O City on the air, shine clear:—

A Pilgrim Soul is drawin' near!

Nae ane can miss the Lan'!
Its trees are green wi' simmer;
Its burns rin glad on every han';
Its sea is bricht wi' glimmer!
Its streets nae Pallid Pain hae trod—
Nae ane can mis the Lan' o' God!

BELOW AND ABOVE.

I.—BELOW.

A City on earth where all is still.

Its streets run through the valleys chill,

And wind all silent acrest the hill,

And all within the City is still.

No labor by any is ever done ;

No deeds of evil are ever begun ;

No acts of kindness from sun to sun.

A City where labor is never done.

No sorrows or tears in heart or eye.

None feel the storm of the pitiless sky.

The wildest hurricane sweepeth by
And never awaketh a fearful cry!

The doors of its homes have never a bell
The coming of outer world to tell;
No sound is heard of joy or of knell;
The doors of its homes have never a bell.

The citizens of this City still,
They never return from valley chill;
And where they entered upon the hill
The citizens all remain there still.

They take no heed of the passing days;
Like miners, they see no sunlight rays;
No clocks sound out Time's changing relays—
They give no heed to the passing days!

And the roofs are brown—but some are green,
And many are flecked with flowers I've seen,

And some have white balustrades, I wean :

And the roofs are brown, and flowered and green.

And all the city is lying asleep—

Its slumber must surely be sound and deep,

For none ever hear the mourners who weep

At the doors of the City all hushed and asleep !

II.—ABOVE.

A City on high where no one dies.

Broad streets are astir in loftiest skies,

Where psalms and hallelujahs arise—

A City all fair where no soul dies !

Where palms are green, and harps are of gold,

Where rivers have run forever of old,

Where glories abide no bard hath told,

With evergreen palms and harps all gold.

Its Hills resound the Great Jubilee—

The people of God from Bondage are free !

O City far off, my soul yearns for thee—

To stand on thy Hills mid God's Jubilee !

Its homes are all " Mansions," many and fair ;

No breath contagious can enter there.

The soul breathes in Celestial air !

Its " Many Mansions " are healthful and fair !

No sorrows—no tears in heart or eye ;

No rains beat down from pitiless sky ;

No hurricane wildly sweeping by—

No sorrows—no tears in heart or eye !

The City is ever awake—ago ;

The River hath ever an onward flow ;

No mourners are weeping, as down below—

The City is ever alive—ago !

Its walls are Jasper, and Gates are Pearl;
Foundations are Emerald, Sapphire, and Beryl.
Never can enemy injury hurl
On Walls of Jasper and Gates of Pearl!

Its roofs immortal are woven of light,
As bright to the sun as day to the night!
Its Sea of Crystal is shimmering bright—
Its roofs immortal are woven of light!

Eternity strikes from all its towers!
Eternity blooms from all its flowers—
Eternity perfumes all its bowers—
Eternity strikes from all its towers!

WITHOUT AND WITHIN.

Without, are sounds of earth :

      Soul-sounds within !

Without, the rolling wheels

Of Traffic, which man feels

Bearing him onward in his strife for gain :

      Voices of grief, or mirth—

      Sounds of the World's great din.

Far other sounds, within !

Within the human soul—

      God speaks within.

Deep questionings are heard ;

The lowest depths are stirred ;
Monitions come from far Eternal Shore !
   Voices, through tears and fears,
   Come from the far off years,
Calling the soul within !

Without, the world's loud call :
   God calls within.
Without, the fleeting toys
Of earthly gold and joys :
Within, Eternity calls souls away.
   A Macedonian cry :
   " Come, help ; we thirst : we die !"
God calls within !

I know my life should be
   Lived from within.
Where men have need the most ;
Where life hath dearest cost ;

Where most I can, there should I go, and stay !

     Into the Cavern Vast,

     The years fly—oh ! so fast,

And are not lived again !

Where God's quick bugle call

     Urge men to stand ;

Where fog-bells dangers show ;

Where warrior trumpets blow,

My soul doth tell me there to take my place.

     Where right is battling Wrong,

     Or weak assailed by strong,

Lend there the weak thy hand !

And Conscience whispers : "shame,"

     Deep down within ;

" Shame, when so great the need,

Lagging with wine and reed,

While God's great army battles sore with sin!''

Nor will it do to say :

"God can the waves all stay : ''

God calls within !

Without, the world doth call !

God calls within !

World-gifts slip swift away :

God's gifts will always stay.

Eternal voices call to thee, O soul.

O soul, attentive be :

Follow eternity :

True life's within !

Babel-cries are without—

God's voice within !

Follow not the worldly shout :

Follow not the cries without.

Live true life, and brave, for men and God.
       Whirlpools are swirling near,
       Roar of breakers thou canst hear !
Hear God within.

THE SILENT BUILDING.

I KINGS VI. 7.

I.

There rose a building beautiful,
    Of costly work and rare !
No hammer's sound—no chisel's click
    Fell on the silent air.
And every column took its place ;
    Each rafter, beam, and sill.
No tool of iron was heard, as rose
    The Temple vast and still.

On Northern Mountains, cedar crowned,
    The fragrant wood was squared ;
And fair veined marbles workmen found,

And oer the seas prepared.
Through centuries vast the trees had grown
    Upon the Syrian Hill
To build the House which rises there
    In majesty, all still.

And fairest gold from Ophir came,
    And jewels from the mine,
To make the wondrous Silent House
    Surpassing fair and fine.
The ships went out which Hiram sent—
    The King's vast fleet came in ;
And Tyre's proud wharves resounded far
    With workmen's noisy din !

But on the Hill of Zion, there,
    Fashioned with skillful hands,
In noiselessness, fair Salem's pride,
    The wondrous Building stands !

Its lofty cornice, cedar roofs,

    Without a sound rose there :

Its altars and its far-famed courts—

    A Palace rich and rare !

II.

Even thus God's hand is building now

    A wondrous House for Him.

He works amid the brightest days,

    And oft mid shadows dim.

Its stately walls He, silent, rears

    Along no earthly shore.

'The topmost stone He soon will lay

    In the Forevermore !

No sound is heard of tool of iron ;

    No chisel's sharp, quick ring ;

No hammer's heavy blow—no ax—

Nor any such a thing.
In silent majesty He builds
  The Temple of the Skies.
Oh! see its walls—its pillars vast,
  In wondrous beauty rise!

Hills of far Lebanon are here ;
  All quarries are below!
Down here on earth, the chisel's click
  And hammer's heavy blow!
The blocks are hewed, the timbers squared,
  The pillars fashioned here.
All work is done this side the Gate—
  No sound falls over there.

And God, the Master Builder, hews :
  He aims each skillful blow :
He walks on Lebanon—He sees
  The quarries dark below.

He chooseth what will suit Him best
For His fair House above.
In deepest mines—on Lebanon—
His tools are used in Love.

God builds on high with human souls!
Cedars from Lebanon,
Gold from the mines of Ophir, or
The marble's polished stone.
Hewn on the hills—from quarries digged
By skillful Hand Divine ;
Polished, and shaped, and fitted here
In the House of Souls to shine!

And many a ship our King doth sail
Upon the wide—wide sea.
Which rolls its waves along the shores
Of far Eternity :
Laden with marble from the mine,

Or cedars from the hill,
He bears them to fair Judah's Land
Some place above to fill.

From noisy mountains God doth take
Pure soul to quietness;
From dark deep mines of doubt and sin
To Land of lasting peace.
In from Life's seas His ships do glide
Bearing them safe to shore,
Silently God fits each in place
To go out nevermore.

O soul of mine, dost feel sometimes
The chisel driveth sore?
Dost think sometimes amid the work
Along earth's Babel shore,
God's ax rings sharp on Lebanon,
His hammer in the mine?

My soul, tis God's wise way to make
    Thee bright in glory shine!

On earth all tools of iron are used.
    Their sounds shall never fall
Where God in New Jerusalem
    Builds up His Palace Wall!
We feel the smart—we suffer now—
    Sometimes are in despair.
God's mallets hurt—God's chisels pain—
    Sweet rest is over there!

O soul of mine, thank God below
    For ax and chisel ring.
Lord, search for us on Lebanon,
    And to Thy Temple bring!
Dig us from out dark mines of sin—
    If ax stroke sharp must fall,
Shape us for place at last to fill

Within Thy Palace Wall!
O Master Builder, canst Thou find
Pure Ophir gold in me?
Cedar of Lebanon, or smooth
Fair marble canst thou see?
A monumental pillar, Lord,
My soul doth long to stand
And tell thy love and wondrous grace
In the Eternal Land!

THE FOREIGNER.

The soul is like a foreigner who wanders up and
    down
The busy streets and thoroughfares of many a
    foreign town,
Hearkening to catch the tuneful words that link
    the soul to home ;
Searching for signs of Father-land wherever he
    doth roam.

I know the world is pleasant with its wondrous
    seas and hills ;
And sometimes its bright landscapes all my heart
    with gladness fills.

Along its broad green river banks, or on its
    flecked lea—
Along its white-lined mountain tops some signs
    of home I see.

Sometimes such wondrous mountains fair, like
    pillars of the skies—
Sometimes such grassy islands greet my wander-
    ing feet and eyes—
Sometimes such crystal rivers run with such a
    crystal flow,
That I am cheated, and I think my home is here
    below !

The blue-bells on their fragile stems nod me a
    welcome fair ;
The hawthorns blossom out their joy ; the daisies
    star-robes wear ;

And forests have a low-voiced moan, like the
    vast swaying sea—
I know that earth is wondrous, but not Father-
    land to me.

For when the sea doth wreck the ships that on
    its storm waves ride—
When snow-drifts from the mountain crests the
    valley hamlets hide—
When crystal rivers rise in rage sweeping their
    banks away,
And frosts nip all the daisies sweet, and night
    enshrouds the day—

When ocean billows cover o'er the islands green
    and fair,
And forests moan the sea-storm's moan, and
    death rides everywhere—

I then feel sure again my soul a foreigner doth
    roam,
And earth, at times so beautiful, is not the spirit's
    home!

The human soul is loyal, and is very willful too!
Like magnet to the Polar Star, the soul is very
    true!
And as it wanders lonesomely the streets all up
    and down,
It feels like foreigner who seeks the Home-land
    shore and town.

North Hermon's peaks are wondrous fair, and
    Judah's hills of green
Bathed with the dews, or gilded with the sun-rays
    shimmering sheen;
But Heavenly dews fall on the Hills Celestial of
    the skies,

And in the Father-land above the sun-light never
    dies !

Such robes of green are on its trees—its flowers
    so wondrous fair
As never island in earth seas, or flower of earth
    can wear!
A River broad and full flows through the City's
    streets above ;
A rainbow spans a great white throne : the City's
    watch-word, " Love."

Horizon lines of snowy crests are but the shores
    to me
That bound the Land I'm longing for beyond the
    restless sea !
And all the streets of cities where I wander up
    and down

But turn me to the Golden Street within the
Heavenly Town.

The forest's moan, the river's flow, the sea storm
or its rest—,
The dark or bright but point me to sweet Beulah
of the Blest.
Oh! when will masts and sails come o'er from
Land far—far away?
How long a foreigner must I in foreign country
stay?

O, Father-land, my heart grows sore—my feet so
long to be
On islands green washed by the waves of thy
clear Crystal Sea?
My ears so long to catch the song thy glorious
choir doth sing?
When will Time's waves my wandering soul into
the Harbor bring?

TWO PILOTS.

Whatever Time doth make of me
That am I in Eternity.
> Life—was it meant for Beauty?
> Life—was it sent for Duty?

In open boat with careless oars
I drift along the greenest shores.
> I hear no call of Duty;
> Life seems to be for Beauty.

My hand holds hard the straining wheel
Where rocks rake sharp the strongest keel.

I see no forms of Beauty ;
Life seems to be for Duty.

Then, is no beauty for the soul,
A runner running for the goal? .
    Is race-course sandy Duty,
    And no green spots of Beauty ?

And does the soul no duty find,
A sailor driven by angry wind?
    Is Life-sea stormless Beauty,
    And no rough waves of Duty?

When in the Harbor at the shore,
And all the sailing time is oer,
    The soul shall see that Beauty
    Was woven here with Duty.

When by the River cool and clear
The soul walks freed from every fear,
10

The soul shall see that Duty
Was woven here with Beauty.

Duty and Beauty urge the soul,
A runner running for the goal.
The soul grows fair by Beauty!
The soul grows strong by Duty!

What we are now that shall we be
Along the great Eternity :
A giant soul by Duty :
A happy soul by Beauty !

Beauty and Duty—which is best ?
One is soul labor—one, soul rest.
Do souls grow most by Beauty ?
Or strengthen most by Duty ?

That soul serves God the very best
Who joins the anxious care and rest—

The deep-lined care of Duty,
The trustful rest of Beauty.

God calls the soul by Duty's ways
Margin to leave for Beauty's praise.
The King hath wedded Beauty
With golden ring to Duty.

Beauty and Duty, Pilots twain
Across the treacherous pathless main
Over to Beulah's boundless plain.
Souls anchor, following Duty.
Souls rest who sail with Beauty.

" A LITTLE WHILE."

JOHN, XVI: 18.

" A little while," I gladly say
And turn my eyes toward coming day,
And mountains rising far away.

" A little while."   Like draw-bridge great
Across the moat of earthly state,
The other end at castle gate !

The deep wide sea we often fear
Becomes the shallow narrow mere—
" A little while " brings shore so near.

" A little while " here down below

Where sorrows have their ebb and flow,
Where souls along the sand bars go—

Amid the fogs on earthly strand
" A little while," as children stand
To see the sun with glass in hand—

Then God will answer soul demands ;
Our hands shall clasp the friendly hands
Which beckon us from Sunny Lands !

Our eyes shall see the sweetest face
In all that glorious, cloudless place,
And glassless each sweet feature trace !

" A little while."   On eagle wings,
The soul flies up to Heavenly things—
No more to earthly stubble clings.

" A little while."   With wind-filled sails

I scud before earth's stormiest gales ;
No stormiest sky my spirit quails !

" A little while." It dries my eyes.
I turn them upward to the skies
Where lifts the Green of Paradise.

I turn away my listening ear—
The Falls of Heavenly Hills I hear,
And Rivers running crystal clear !

" A little while " and I shall see
The City where I long to be,
And plains of bright Eternity.

" A little while !" I well can wait
A patient pilgrim near the Gate,
Along the earth-street called: "The Strait."

I know the Hills of Paradise—

I know the square-built Walls will rise
Ere long upon my happy eyes!

LED.

PSALM CVII: 7.

Lonely and almost forsaken, I stand amid Doubt's
  dreary twilight.

Scarcely the outlines of City I long for appear in
  the distance.

Loud at times on the sea-shore waves dash music discordant—

Echoing voices resounding far from the Past's
  haunted caverns!

Dim eddies of swirling Belief are circling around
  in confusion!

Faith is a Pilotless sea-wave, its strength on an
  unknown shore wasting:

Or else like a poor eyeless bird, striking wings
    'gainst the walls of dumb cavern!

I'm almost fearing to fear amid these wave-beats
    incessant—

Almost hopeless of Hope, tossed sailless on
    Doubt's trackless ocean!

Raindrop high in the cloudland swept by the
    stress of the Storm King—

Snowflake down through the air-land lost amid
    millions more swirling—

Skiff in the wildest commotion of ocean by hurri-
    cane driven,

Might chatter of shore or of rest, as wisely as my
    restless spirit!

Raindrops and white helpless snow-flakes are not
    poor orphan-like wanderers.

Storm-clouds and every wind-current have Hand
   behind them, controlling.
My soul on the dreariest ocean, when all seems
   certain destruction,
Like rain-drop high in empyrean by some Hand
   surely is guided!

Blindfolded, if led by the Wisest, is better than
   Ignorance seeing.
Darkness is better than daylight when hand is in
   hand of Omniscience.
Better than all helpers else is He, the Omnipotent
   Helper,
Opening all doorways before me and swinging all
   gateways for passing.

Sometimes I fancy the burdens, the grief, and the
   Future's sealed silence—

All the deep purpose unfathomed along which
my soul-life is running,

Best are and sweetest, remembering the one loving Friend of the straying

Whose footsteps of bitterest sorrow up Calvary
weary went bleeding.

My heart that hath been like a sea wave contin-
ually seeking a landing

Hath touched a home shore in the knowing that
changes both good and ill-seeming

Are ordered by Infinite Love from the bosom of
Infinite Wisdom.

The rain-drops and snow-flakes find Harbor—and
so doth my soul in His loving !

WATCHING.

I.

All through the weary night
A watcher watched for day!
The minutes went with slow delay.
At last, the night was streaked with gray!
The weary watcher raised his eyes,
And saw the day-dawn streak the skies—
He saw 'the sun spears pierce the skies!
At last the night turned into day.
And fields of green
And golden sheen
Broke on the watcher's weary sight!

Man has no hand to drive
One leaden, weary hour.
Time onward swings by God's great power.
Man's place, to do—to watch—to wait:
God backward swings the long-shut gate!
As ocean spares a flake of snow
Amid its restless ebb and flow,
So God needs not our feeble state.
  O watch His Will!
  Work, soul: be still!
Live following God : so *shalt* thou live.

  When at the noon of night
  The dawn seems far away,
And Hope's strong foot hath gone astray,
And in the soul no blessings stay ;
Faith walketh far adown the Skies
And seeth Towers and Walls arise—
And Heavenly Hosts in bright array—

Till gloom of noon of night all dies;
        And, more and more,
        The green, glad Shore
Breaks on the watcher's weary sight!

        When Night grows old and gray,
        And Day-Spring, close at hand,
Begins to outline sea and land —
What wave-sounds swell on every hand!
And swift across the twilight bar,
.Light-sails, as soft as fancies are,
Come in from seas of night to land.
        How blest from Night
        To sail to Light—
From vigils dark to greet the Day!

                II.

        All through Time's weary night
        Soul watcher watched for day.

The years crept past with slow delay.

At last, Time's night was streaked with gray!

The weary watcher raised his eyes,

And lo! God's day-dawn streaked the skies—

He saw gold sun spears pierce the skies!

At last Time's Night brought Heavenly Day.

  The City Fair

  Rose on the air;

And visions bright broke on his sight!

  As years grew old and gray

  Along the Border Land—

When God's sweet rest was close at hand;

Sounds came no soul could understand.

And, swift across Death's sandy bar,
On whitest sails without a fear

He went from seas of Night to Land.

  In from Time's Night

  He sailed to Light—

The soul-ship greeted Port of Day!

  Worth watching, toiling here ;
  Worth drifting—shifting now,
To feel at last the joyous prow
Touch Heavenly Strand!—worth tossings now !
Life surges cannot beat so sore
To keep believing soul from shore.
Watch, soul, mid Ocean's angry roar :
Harbor's in sight! Storms beat no more!
  On tideless sea
  How sweet to be!
Souls leave the watch deck over there !

IRON GATES.

ACTS, XII. 10.

Fear not, bound heart.

God can strike off each iron chain ;

God can strike off each gnawing pain ;

And loose thee from each bitter smart.

In prison cell,

Chained to the Roman men of war,

An Angel opened Peter's door,

And showed him light, unspeakable.

And past the band,

And past each dreary dungeon ward,

11

And past the sleeping Roman guard,
Was Peter led by Angel hand.

As if it knew
The presence of the Mighty Lord,
The Iron Gate, of free accord,
Swung backward to the prisoner's view !

What to our Lord
Can Herods do with all their hate ?
And what are chains, and Iron Gate,
And bolted wards, and sharpest sword ?

The Iron Gates
Of Grief and Sorrow, black as night,
Hide cities fair, and joys from sight.
No hinge upon its pivot grates !

And sore and bound,
Our hearts lie captive as we grope .

For open doors and hills of hope,
And think, nor doors nor hopes are found.

What to our Lord
Are Iron Gates of hopeless Grief?
He brings a sweet and swift relief,
And open doors, with slightest word!

From strongest walls—
From deepest dungeons of despair,
He leads us to the City Fair,
Where blessed sunlight on us falls.

Unquestioning,
When such a Guide before us goes,
And His strong arm around us throws,
The Iron Gates do backward swing!

And, by God's grace,
Each trusting heart shall safely pass

All bolted doors and gates of brass,

And reach, at length, an " Open Place."

Our dearest Lord

Will lead us up the Heavenly Way.

The Gate of Everlasting Day

Will open of "its own accord!"

FATAL LACKS.

A house may lack an ornament or two
           And be secure.
           Will it endure
When storms do drive and winds do blow and rains
Beat heavily 'gainst doors and window panes,
      If only shifting sands,
      And not foundation stones
Be laid beneath its walls?
             Will sand grains do?

An arch may lack an ornament or two
           And still not fall.
           But give it all

The other stones of power, or usefulness,
Or beauty; and then lack but this:—
    The Key-Stone! Will the rest
    Be held each one in place?
        Will such lack do?

A ship may lack a mast, a sail, or two,
        Nor be a wreck!
        And from its deck
May miss a cable or an anchor chain,
And not go down within the stormy main.
    But if a plank be gone
    Beneath the water line—
        Will such lack do?

Your child may lack a ring, a dress, or two;
        And its sweet smile
        Your cares beguile.
But if it lack the seeing, hearing, when

You kiss its cheek, and call its name!—what then?
　　　If life be lacking there
　　　From that sweet form so fair—
　　　　　Will all else do?

So man may lack in life a thing or two:
　　　　　May lack a name
　　　　　Well known to fame—
May have no home, nor wealth, nor power!—
What if he lack God's air a single hour?
　　　　Will gold, or acres fair—
　　　　Will home, or friendships dear?
　　　　　Will all else do?

A human soul may lack a joy or two!
　　　　　Lack happiness
　　　　　In world like this;
And not go down shipwrecked in dangerous sea!
What if its very life-breath lacking be?

How shall it then pursue

These shoals and quick-sands through ?

Will such lack do ?

A human being stands along the shore ;

A pathless main

Swells wide between

His feet and foreign land, thousands of miles

away ;

No ship—no sail on all the stormy sea !

Can mortal man cross oer

The stormy ocean's roar

From shore to shore ?

O soul of mine, is lack like this to you ?

Heaven hidden lies

Beyond the skies ;

And thou art standing on Time's distant shore.

Only God's spirit can transport thee oer !

On sea unknown and vast,

Thou lackest God's great grace !—

    Will such lack do ?

REWARDS.

I SAM. 30: 24

" Gird on your swords for battle—
But some take care of the train,
And watch the weak and weary
Till the army returneth again.
The soldier that fighteth the battle,
The soldier that guardeth the train
Shall be alike rewarded
When the army returneth again."

King David spake at Ziglag :
The warriors hurried o'er ;
Two hundred footsore and fainting

Remained on the other shore.

When Amalek's bands were routed,

And the Hebrew captives saved,

Those watching the stuff were sharers

With those who the battle braved.

" Gird on your swords for battle,

Some stay with the ambulance train,

Some trudge behind all weary,

Some patiently suffer pain.

The soldier that fighteth the battle,

The soldier that guardeth the train,

Shall be alike rewarded

When the King returneth again."

King David's Son commanded,

The warriors hurry away ;

And many at Besor weary

And footsore and fainting stay.

When God's foes all are vanquished,
The captives returned and saved,
Those watching behind shall be sharers
With those who the battle braved.

I sometimes think by the brookside :
'Tis easier far to stand
At the front where battle is hottest,
With dangers on every hand ;
Than to watch the stuff at Besor,
Or patiently suffer and bear !
For it suiteth the cry of my spirit
The warrior's armor to wear !

But the King goes up from Ziglag
And biddeth me here to stay.
I'll keep sharp watch for His coming
With army from stormy fray.
I cherish His faithful promise

To weak ones left behind :
The warriors alike with the watchers
A portion at last shall find."

Some souls can scale the summits ;
Some hands can hold the helm ;
But some must stand in shadows
Of mountains that overwhelm !—
Or only swing in the hammock
That's rocked by the angry blast !
How sweet to think that the sailors
Shall all reach Harbor at last !

The souls on loftiest mountains
From Home are as far away
As those who in valley shadows
In the mists and darkness stay.
For the Cross of Christ is ever
The Door to the City for all ;

And the bravest soul must enter
Alike with the weak and small.

It may be for me sweeter
To camp on the Upper Plains
On a line with tents of soldiers
Because of my Besor pains.
I hear at the front the war-cry—
The battle is well begun!
How sweet when the war is ended
All the army to hear: *"well done!"*

" FOLLOW ME."

MATT. IV 19.

O hast thou never seen, sore heart,

Some glimpses of that sweetest face,

Or felt that presence make thy place

Of crowded ills, by His sweet grace,

A Holy Place—a Bethel place?

    Hast thou not seen the Christ, sore heart?

O hast thou never touched, sick heart,

His glorious garment-hem?   What thrill

Stirred tumult in thy blood's sick chill

When He looked—bidding thee stand still!

What health the sickly soul did fill!

    Hast touched Christ's garment hem, sick heart?

O hast thou followed Him, sad heart,

In olive-clad Gethsemanes

Amid the solemn agonies

Of midnight glooms and soul-wrung cries

Which sorrowed earth and thrilled the skies?

  O hast thou followed him, sad heart?

Or hast thou climbed the heights, glad heart;

Hast been with Him up Tabor Hill?

Hast seen the glow of glory fill

His sacred form, and felt the still

Sweet calm of Heaven thy soul-life thrill?

  Hast climbed the Tabor Heights, glad heart?

Along Gennesar's shore, lone heart,

When night of useless toil was oer

And boat swung idly to the shore

And disappointment made thee sore,

(How lone and still the day-break shore!)

Hast thou not met with Him, lone heart?

Or when dread storm, bereaved heart,

Swept some dear treasure in the sea

Of boundless sealed Eternity,

Hast thou not seen rough Galilee

Crouch at His feet, a quiet sea?

Hast met Christ in the storm, sad heart?

Oh! weary days we 've had, my heart?

And to my tear-dimmed, vacant eyes

Each blessing wore a dark disguise!

He came; and with a soft surprise

The light crept oer my spirit's skies,

And Day-spring came from God, my heart!

Like warmth of Spring-time, waiting heart—

Like rainbow on the storm—like land

To shiprecked souls—like home-land shore

To exiles—like strong rescuing hand

12

To sinking spirit—rest and land,
　Salvation, home is Christ, tried heart!

　"Come follow me." Yes go, dear heart.
Thine ear shall hear the gladsome cheer
Of Paradise; the sweet surprise
Of Heavenly glory greet thine eyes!
All dreary foam of weary fear
　Breaks on the reefs of Death, dear heart!

Fear not to follow Him, tired heart.
Bend low to trace where He hath trod.
He came from God and went to God.
Oer lawns of joy and grave-yard sod—
At last through River deep and broad,
　He'll lead thee to thy rest, tired heart!

LIFE'S LOOM.

I sit at the Wheel of Life to spin ;

    And yet no spinner am I.

I stand at the Gate to enter in,

    And yet poor sinner am I.

The threads seem tangled and which to choose

    Who'll guide me as I spin ?

The Gate is shut and hard to loose —

    Who'll open and let me in ?

Oh ! how the beautiful web to flower

    With beautiful tints who'll tell ?

Oh ! where shall I find Omnipotent Power

To break this sinful spell?

The fabric I weave must ever endure,

For fadeless threads I spin:

If the Gate swings open my heart is sure

There is Life Eternal within!

Some days at the Loom the threads fly fast

And slowly they creep some days;

Like the years of Life, some winging past,

And some on wheels of delays!

The warp and the woof are sometimes blurred

By the spinner's tears who spins!

The sea of the soul is sometimes stirred

By Euroclydons of sins!

But slow or fast, in the dark or sun,

The web in the Loom still grows;

And rapid or slow Life's race is run,

And the hour-glass sand still flows.

My hand that holds the shuttle of Life,

    Must hurry it through and through.

My heart that strives in bitterest strife

    Must carry its burdens too.

The human soul must weave its web,

    And the human hand must do.

Eternity guides the silvery thread

    And weaves it through and through.

And the delicate fabric woven now

    Will be a robe immortal;

And the journey we go will lead the soul

    Within the City's portal.

And the wondrous web I try to fill

    With a beautiful golden filling;

In trial's hour my heart holds still,

    And my soul is strong and willing.

I sigh sometimes when threads do break—

Life's threads will snap asunder!
And the human heart has many an ache,
   For the human hands will blunder!

I sit at the Wheel of Life and spin,
   And yet no spinner am I.
I knock at the Gate to enter in,
   And yet poor sinner am I.
An unseen Spinner is guiding my hand
   And choosing the threads I spin ;
An unseen Friend beside me doth stand
   And open and let me in.

My heart grows glad at the Loom of Life—
   The shuttle doth cheerfully go.
I feel an end of the weary strife—
   Life-waters have musical flow.
Will my fabric suit the Spinner on high ?
   Will it cover my deathless soul ?

Shall I enter the City beyond the sky,

    And be crowned at Life's far goal?

One day the woof will all be run;

    The warp will all be filled.

One day the journey will all be done,

    And the noisy wheel be stilled!

Life's dusty Loom shall silent stand,

    Life's busy shuttle stay.

The Pilgrim shall enter the Heavenly Land,

    And the Spinner have resting day.

SHELLS.

Far inland from the restless sea
In softest tinted shell-home caught,
I hear the ocean monody
With hidden caverns' voices fraught.
The restless tides where memory rides
Rise, ebb and moan through sea-shell lone!

What strange sea-voices float anear!
I swing in hammock 'neath the mast.
The ripple of the waves I hear.
With canvas reefed and anchors cast
I see the sail and hear the hail :
"Ho! ship ahoy!" with heartfelt joy!

I listen on my sea-shell shore
'Till Harbor Bar is past ; and home
Beyond the ocean's billowy roar
Greets me, and I no longer roam !
My charmed eyes with glad surprise
See glorious towers and radiant bowers.

So, far away from that clear sea
Of crystal, washing Heavenly strand,
I catch the wondrous melody
In soul-shell fair here far inland.
Eternal swells, soul's echoing shells
Catch full and clear in earth lands drear !

What wondrous sounds within the
soul—A sea shell wrought by hands
above ! Waves after waves of music roll
Within its caverns ; song of love,
Like white ship, glides adown its tides ;

And harps rejoice with harper's voice!

I almost feel the spray of waves
Cooling my cheek.!   I almost see
The Harbor oer the gulf of graves !
I almost feel the liberty
Of Heavenly plains ! Oh ! wondrous strains—
Sea mystery by soul-shell sea !

What cheer I hear from that far shore !
I rest with anchors firmly cast.
All soul-sails reefed—all dangers o'er—
All sounds of rocks, storm-washed, are past.
The tuneful rote of sea wave's note
The soul-shells beat, and Pain's retreat.

No bridges span the distance vast
From time to the Eternal Shore.
No dark complaints can anchor cast

Within the Bay Supernal.   Or

What sails can reach that shining beach ?

What thoughts can pry the Future's sky ?

As dew drop small reflects the sky ;

As shell of ocean speaks its roar ;

My soul-shell sounds the Bye-and-bye,

And soft reflects the Hither shore ;—

An earnest sweet that I shall greet

Eternally the shore and sea !

Oer intoned bridges free I go

To heights above from this lone plain.

These are the transports which below

Leave earth and shores of Glory gain.

Faith sails this way from night to day—

Hope's chiming bells wake notes of shells.

I hearken on my soul-shell shore

'Till I can hear the anchor fall

Far—far away the ocean o'er,

Beneath the Heaven-built Jasper Wall ;

Where countless sails, beyond all gales,

Are furled at last, soul anchors cast !

THE KING.

In Florence, city beautiful, there stands
Within the Pitti Palace all alone
A wondrous statue carved from purest stone ;
And round the wall are mirrors on all hands,
Within whose constant gaze the statue stands.

In Heaven, the City Beautiful above,
Within the Crystal Palace of the skies,
The central gaze of all the countless eyes
Within the realms of glory and of love,
Within His Palace stands the King above.

And all His universe is mirror clear,

Reflecting Him on every hand ; you trace

The sweetest lineaments of form and face

In all His works and ways, afar and near ;

While in His subjects' love He shines most clear.

Fair Florence o'er the seas is village small,

And Pitti Palace but a hut of clay

In the compare of City far away

With gates of pearl and glittering diamond wall !

Earth's largest city in its light seems small !

I ofttimes long to see in foreign lands—

In Pitti Palace or in Louvre Halls,

The works of Masters making dumbest walls

Speak out and answer all the soul demands :

Michael and Raphael speaking through the lands.

One's soul must sure expand beneath the Dome

Of great St. Paul's—or kindle with strange fire

While gazing up at each white fretted spire

Of fair Milan—or like a pilgrim roam

In vaulted naves beneath St. Peter's Dome.

Louvre or Pitti or Cathedral vast

Of Paul or Peter—all the fretted spires

Of fair Milan, lit with the sunset fires—

All works of Angelo or Raphael past

Seem shadows dim on Heaven's clear glory cast!

How pilgrim souls do long to see that Form

In Central Palace of the loftiest skies !

The cynosure of all Heaven's myriad eyes,—

The sunlight of the City, clear and warm—

The rainbow glory of receding storm !

He wakes the songs eternal singers sing ;

Heaven's harpers harping harp His wondrous
　　love !

He is the light and joy of land above—

The Maker making every glorious thing!

I join the song celestial singers sing!

THE GATE BEAUTIFUL.

I would not live a selfish life ;
I scarce can breathe this stifling air !
Each dreary hour is a weary strife
After a better and higher life.
I am sure that beyond such narrow life,
O Lord, Thy pastures are green and fair !
I lie to-day at the Beautiful Gate
Which leadeth to life more true and great.

     Open, O Lord, thy Beautiful Gate ;
     Open the Gate to me—
          Even unworthy me!

I know that life is purer far,

And holier than my heart has found.

Beyond the dark full many a star

Lights up its paths—shows where we are!

Outside the Gate is never a star!

A captive in chains, poor, blind, and late,

My heart to-day pleads, Lord, with Thee:

" Oh! open the Beautiful Gate to me:

      Open Thy Gate to me—

            Even unworthy me ! "

Beyond this selfish life there lies

A Life of Faith with meaning true.

There are toils, and tears, and work to do—

True souls live there, why cannot you?

Their words and deeds make deserts to bloom,

And wilderness places to blossom: the tomb

Of the human soul gives up its dead:

For Idol Gods, the Cross instead

Is melting, and moulding the world anew!

This is the work that others can do,

And why not you?—

      " Open, O Lord, the Beautiful Gate,

      Open Thy Gate to me—

            Even unworthy me!

This world is not a dreary waste;

This world is still our Master's home.

For, when He turns on me His eye,

My heart's low walls seem vast and high;

My work-house rises and reaches the sky;

Its dingy walls become a dome;

And its weary labor a gracious task

Yielding me more than heart could ask.

Whenever He opens the Beautiful Gate

This Life expands to Temple great,

And feels to the heart like home!

Open, dear Lord, the Beautiful Gate—
Open Thy Gate to me—

Even unworthy me !

Thy love lights earth like morning ;
And the tides of sunshine flow
From out Thy presence to gladden the sea,
And make all the earth speak plainly of Thee,
Till praise, like an ocean, rolls backward to Thee !
All Nature gives praises to God the Great !
But I, with a tongue, still, cold, and dumb,
All crippled and tired and very late,
Weary and footsore, to-day here wait.
My soul pleads only its need of Thee !

Open, O Lord, the Beautiful Gate—
Open Thy Gate to me—

Even unworthy me !

I am waiting—so weary waiting

For Hope and for Love from Thee.

I have come from afar, O Lord, to feel

Thy life-giving Love and influence steal

Through heart and through soul my being to
    thrill!

I have crept and tottered with failing strength,

And here I lie at Thy Gate, at length.

Oh! open it wide! Let me feel the sun

Shine full on my soul; and with new-life begun,

I will give that life with its love to Thee.

        Open, O Lord, the Beautiful Gate—

        Open Thy Gate to me—

           Even unworthy me!

The Gate swings wide on its hinges—

The Beautiful Gate swings wide!

From depths of untold glory what light

Streams on my soul! All clouds of the Night

Drive fast away! What glory and light,

Rolling their floods in a boundless tide

Out through the Gateway, swinging wide!

And, coming from Life's fair hills, I feel

The breath of Love and of duty steal

Over my soul with a strange, sweet thrill.

Open stands the Beautiful Gate—

Open, dear Lord, to me—

Even unworthy me!

I enter into Thy pastures wide;

I find new duties; I gain new strength.

My tongue is not dumb; and here at length

I am not a cripple—borne down by the tide!

O soft cool winds that around me blow!

O River of Life with thy crystal flow!

O Love unfathomed, which none can know!

My soul is afloat on the boundless tide

Which flows through the Gateway, swinging
    wide!

O Lord, I thank Thee, Thy Beautiful Gate

Stands open now to me—

Even unworthy me !

Yet still I ask Thee for one thing more—

With a trusting heart I ask :

Beyond this Beautiful Gate my soul

Would find its fairest and truest goal—

Freedom from Sin !   Let no veil fall

Between its life and Thee.   From the thrall

Of Sin, O Lord, deliver me.

And through the Beautiful Gate, swung wide,

May Mercy and Love meet my soul in a tide

That shall bring me home to Thee.

O Beautiful Gate,

Swing wide—swing wide.

Stand open thus to me—

Even unworthy me !

TENT AND DWELLING.

2 COR. V: 1.

Winds are beating, storms are breaking
On Life's Tabernacle, making
Rafters creak!   The beams are shaking!

All the wind-strained cords are starting;
All the Tent's worn seams are parting;
All the earth-stakes are upstarting!

And some unseen hand is lifting
Off this Tent!   Low winds are drifting
It away.   Earth scenes are shifting!

When breaks down this Tent so mortal,
When winds creak through many a portal,
We shall find a Roof Immortal.

Even here, through broken ceiling,
Come swift sun-rays downward stealing,
Glimpses of far joy revealing!

There are fields forever vernal;
There are Mansions fair, eternal,
In the land of light, supernal.

Where the soul doth never borrow
Cares from some unknown to-morrow;
Where the present has no sorrow.

And a crystal sea, whose breaking
No sad dissonance is making—
Soul foundations never shaking.

Where a City's wondrous portal
Breaketh on the soul immortal—
O to pass its Pearly Portal!

When this Tent is sorely shaking —
When the storms its cords are breaking—
When its rafters all are quaking—

When its canvas old is parting—
When its earth-set stakes are starting—
And its seams, by winds, are parting—

When Death's unseen hand is lifting
Off this Tent, and winds are drifting
It away—when all is shifting—

Blessed thought!   The soul hath Dwelling
Far above tumultuous welling
Of earth-waters, madly swelling!

And this mortal turns immortal

When it passes that bright Portal

Of the City fair, immortal!

ALMIGHTY WINGS.

PS. XCI: 4.

When souls are drifted from the land
By earth-winds hard to understand ;
When shore-lines of the soul are gone
And nothing left to fasten on ;
From all Life's dark and dubious things
Take shelter neath the Almighty Wings.

When mid the din and smoke of fight
The heavens are blotted out of sight,
O soul pressed down by Summer's heat,
With fainting heart and weary feet,
Oer stones that hurt and thorn that stings

Press under the Almighty Wings.

When some great soul forgets its trust
And trails its Heaven-wrought robes in dust;
And human faith in human kind
Is shaken sore by some sharp wind,
The soul to God securely clings
And hides beneath the Almighty Wings.

O erring ones, gone forth to try
If earth's fair hills are lifted dry ;
Like Noe's dove to seek a flight
Far out upon the dreary night—
Waste covers still all earthly things !
Come back beneath the Almighty Wings!

Sweet comfort is it thus to find
A covert from each angry wind.
Sweet thought to souls so needing rest

To find such sure, safe, feathery nest :—
From all earth's sins, and cares and stings
To fly beneath the Almighty Wings !

When Life grows dark, and Faith grows
    dim,
No doubts in us can alter Him.
The Pole Star changes not though night
May hide it from the mariner's sight.
My soul to God forever clings.
O cover me, Almighty Wings !

DEPTHS.

Who sees through deep waters the track of the
    keel?
Who sees on Life-sands trace of sorrow I feel?
There are scars on the soul nigh despairing
From the cross—hidden cross I am bearing!

Who sees the high fountains of drops of the rain?
Who sees the deep well-heads of Joy or of Pain?
Who measureth others' heart sadness?
Who soundeth another's heart gladness?

No lead with its sea-line God giveth to thee
To fathom the depths of my soul's restless sea!

On the surface, no signs of commotion—
Wreck and death at the bottom of ocean !

You see no dark cloud on the far happy sky ;
You see no sad tear-trace on face or in eye :
So you say :   " Life is sunshine—not raining !"
While the soul in its pain is complaining !

Who judges correctly of other men's ways ?
They name the Joy, Pain ; they call the Curse,
      Praise !
The Psalms of the soul they call sadness ;
Soul-Requiem name they soul-gladness !

The Law Giver's rod in the time long ago,
From flintiest rock caused cool river to flow :
And, striking through cold rocky sadness,
God calleth up sweet streams of gladness !

The souls that are dragging the Cross oer the
　　sand,

Will stand all erect with bright Crown in God's
　　Land !

The Future's fair page I am reading

Through thorn-pangs which cause me soul bleed-
　　ing.

But what the lost treasures of other hearts be—

What fleet has been scattered—what ships
　　wrecked at sea—

What lamps have died down with the burning

While watching for sails ne'er returning—

Or what the heart solitudes deep down below

The stir of the trees where the life-breezes blow,

What reefs lie just under this shining,

Omniscience alone is divining !

Sweet Charity's white silent sail should be known
　　14

On the ocean of other men's souls, all alone.

Sweet Charity saileth so kindly :

Sweet Charity saileth so blindly :

Sweet Charity's keel skimmeth lightly :

Sweet Charity's wake shineth brightly !

HEIGHTS.

My soul has struggled long to climb
Up from the crowded lanes and mirksome air,
Up to the heights by many a winding stair—
I stand to-day on mountain top sublime!

Men say the valleys of the sea
Are deep below as hills of earth are high :
I only know that up from depths my cry
Has climbed the steeps where now I stand so free.

I look down on the world below :
The distance great has covered all its scars.
I upward gaze, and God's bright solemn stars
With even tread, like armies, onward go!

And here between the earth and sky,

A silence falls which makes the height sublime !

The soul feels God which mountain summits
　　climb ;

And all the angry passions hush and die.

I look far down the Eastward side.

The fair green hills and woods of earth I see ;

And many spots well-known and loved by me ;

And quiet seas where white-winged memories
　　ride.

I gaze adown the Westward slope.

A River rapid sweepeth ever by ;

Beyond are mountains lost in bluest sky ;

And far away are breezy Hills of Hope !

And when across from hill to hill

I cast my eye, a Country broad and fair,

With streams and palms and glories everywhere,
And ships at anchor in the Harbor still!

And since I've gained this sweet Upland
The moan of reefs and wave-washed rocks is
      past:
And thunderous tones of far off sorrow's blast
Reach not these heights where, Faith brought,
      now I stand!

The heights of earth outside the Gate—
They are sublime but not the soul's safe home.
Along their crest immortals still might roam,
And freeze with cold upon their high estate!

The vastest outlook is too small
Which takes not in Eternity's fair Plain.
And all the landscape gives the soul but pain,
When shut around by earth's cold, stony wall.

But over there along the skies—
There far away amid the boundless stars,
I see in outline City walls and bars,
And Heights Eternal where none ever dies.

And as one sees from earthly hill
A broader landscape than from earthly plain ;
So my horizon widens when I gain
The Heights sublime which all my longings fill ?

And one glad day I'll pass the walls
Of City Fair—Eternal Hills I'll climb,
And see the King and view the Throne Sublime,
And walk the Plains where endless sunlight falls !

RULE.

PROV. XVI: 32.

Who takes a city old and strong

Mid cannon's roar and whistling balls

And warrior's shout and maddening throng,

Storming the ramparts—scaling walls,

Is Captain mighty, near and far—

Crowned with the Crown—starred with the star !

Because the weaker by the strong

Is vanquished, give him palm and song !

There is a nobler, fiercer strife !

A City walled and full of foes,

Astir with passions darkening life,

Adown whose streets an army goes

To man each breach along the walls:
To guard wherever trumpet calls!
And at its head a Leader tried
Upon a warrior's horse doth ride!

Greater than he who scales a wall
And breaks a city's ramparts through,
Is he who answers God's quick call
And storms this foe with spirit true.
More honors to the soul belong,
Entering the lists against the wrong —
More glory conquering inner foes
Than Prince or Emperor ever knows!

Thy kingdom is within; and know
That there, along the noisy streets
Within the soul, the strongest foe
The truest warrior daily meets!
To drive the wrong from such a Land

Calls for God's help and conquering hand.
Ally thy weakness to God's power—
Storm the black ramparts now—this hour !

Oh ! could we hear the tramp of feet—
The marching of the squadron's there
Along the soul's imperiled street,
How soon we 'd seek His help in prayer !
And where Sin's darkest ramparts frown—
Where Satan dares us beat them down—
Under the blackest frowning wall
The soul on God would quickly call !

His is the greatest fight who wins
The unseen Kingdom of the Soul :
More glory his where fight begins,
And greenest laurels at the goal !
He rules with wider rule whose hand
Sways sceptre of the Inner Land,

Than any King : to him belongs
The Crown who wages war with wrongs.

And one good day the marching feet,
The din of Passion's troops, the tramp
Of Sin's battalions through the street,
The noisy strife of Wrong's black camp—
All shall be hushed for me within :
The war, the strife, the battle's din !
And from His Throne the King come down
And crown me with the victor's crown !

SHELTER.

There's mony a wee sweet daisy sair nipped
   wi' the cold ;
There's mony a cannie sparrow fa's upon the
   bleakie wold ;
The winds hae aft times killit we birdies on the
   tree ; —
But He will gaither in His nest weak bairns like
   you an' me.

The burns rin glad in Simmer, but are dumb in
   Wintry day ;
And what was gleefu' music ance, is ice anent
   the way ;

We canna spier for sadness noo, sae icy cold's
    the heart;
But swift His feathery wings droop roun' and
    warmth and life impart.

The bending heather i' the field, the primrose
    doun the brae,
The hawthorne fragrant i' the glen, and ilka
    milk-white slae,
He sifts His biting frosts upon, and wings His
    blasts wi' cold;
But He gently shields his lamies a' within His
    safe warm fold.

When hawk wi' dark wings swoopeth adoun the
    Simmer sky,
The mither ca's an' frichtened brood aneath her
    wingies fly;

When shadows, swooping, fa' on thee—warld-
    sorrows, trouble-stings—
He ca's for frichtened, troubled souls to rin
    aneath His wings !

The warld maun hae its dangers and its winged
    blasts o' care ;
Yet owre the Desert Elim Palms rise feathery,
    green and fair.
We gang to fin' a City where we hope wi' joy to
    sing ;
And our pilgrim heads are sheltered safe aneath
    His feathery wing.

Amang the mists we stimble and the thunder
    drops fa' fast,
And nicht comes doun upon us wi' nae starlicht
    on the blast !

But nae sparrow e'er escapeth His watchfu' kind-
    ly e'e,
And His gentle wings come droopin' doun to
    shelter you and me.

Wha 's on before wi' bleeding feet atween me an'
    the storm ?
My shield by day, my guide by night—that meek
    an' weary Form ?
Each burden that my heart doth bend, He first
    the burden bore ;
And His guid han' will lead me safe the last dark
    River oer !

The gold comes frae the furnace, and the corn
    doth cease to grin';
The calms are cradles o' the storms, and oceans
    quiet fin'.

We dinna ken how soon may fa' upon our hearts
    sae sair,

Doun frae the Gowden Gate the cry : " *Ye need*
    nae journey mair ! "

Our hopes shall brichten by the way as still we
    forrit gang !

The road rins owre the steep rough hills—it
    winna be for lang !

As Shepherd leads his lamies and ca's them a' by
    name,

Our Frien' will open wide the Gate an' bid us a'
    come hame.

TRANSITION.

The winds were whistling through the sails—
Angry and hungry, heartless gales !
The shore-bound cordage, strand by strand,
Snapped, loosening from the midnight land.
The ship at last to sea quick sped—
Darkness around and storm ahead !

      O, whither bound, frail sail,
      In such an angry gale ?

The crystal water's tuneful rote,
Like music's sweetest, restful note,
Washes the grassy, quiet shore—

Throbs on the Land Forevermore.

Here in the Harbor, anchor cast,

A ship lies swaying, seas all past!

      Touched Land at break of day.

      From earth-shores far away.

Embarking for the last strange sail!

Death-winds are sweeping stormy gale;

And every strand my life doth tie

Loosening! The hour has come to die!

Out quick to sea my spirit fled—

The Known behind—Unknown, ahead!

      What shore, my soul, for thee

      Beyond this midnight sea?

The wavering shadows disappear:

Pain's low susurras beat not here.

This disembarking—oh! how sweet!

How soft this strand to weary feet!

15

The cares that pitched their tents in Time
Never encamp in this bright Clime.

> My soul at dawn of day
> Reached shore here far away.

Transition strange!   From sea to shore!
No sounds I ever heard before:
No sights mine eyes have ever seen:
Such wondrous hills of wondrous green—
Such odorous waves from groves of balm—
Savannas treeless, broad and calm!

> No dissonant clangor breaks
> Oer Heaven's broad inland lakes.

The restless heart of earth-sea beats
Below.   I walk the Golden Streets
On Heavenly Shore, in City free,
Here by this tideless Crystal Sea.

No ocean fogs pitch tents above :
No sea-storms sweep the sky of love.

      Transition strange and sweet,
      Such landing-place to meet !

THE PEACE GIVER.

JOHN XIV: 24.

I.

It was a wild and stormy sea ;

No place of safety left to me.

My little bark was frail and tossed

And I had given up for lost.

A gleam of light gleamed through the storm,

And on the waves a Living Form.

I was afraid so close to be

To such a Being on the sea !

" Be not afraid," He said, " Tis I :"

And Jesus my dear Lord was nigh.

With Him a sweet peace came to me

Upon that wild and stormy sea !

II.

It was a straight and narrow way ;

Now through the night—now through the day.

Footsore and weary up the height

I struggled on through day and night.

And heavy laden I did press

On 'neath my load of weariness.

I doubted whether t' were the road

That God's dear people e'er had trod.

A Pilgrim joined me—spake to me,

And held sweet converse by the way.

My heart was warmed ; my feet so sore

I felt not as I felt before.

And to my soul so glad and light

The Emmaus Town was soon in sight.

At eventide He left me there,

But that straight way seemed passing fair.

And in my soul for weariness

Was left the sweetest rest and peace.

III.

It was a river cold and fleet ;
Upon the brink I pressed my feet.
The yonder shore I strained to see—
No ferryman appeared to me.
And I must go alone to try
The chilling river rushing by !
The skies were growing dark ; the sun
Was setting ; all the day was done.
The hills and sights along this shore
My dimming eyes could see no more.
The voices of this side sank low ;
The day was done, and I must go.
How deep—how cold—how swift the River
Cutting the Now from the Forever !
But when within the stream, a hand

Grasped mine and led me safe to land.

A rod and staff were given to me

To lean upon and be my stay.

And now *that* shore seems dim and far ;

And now *this* shore is bright and near.

All tumult past—the sounds have died

That filled my soul on yonder side.

And fears have ceased, and sin is past—

My feet have reached this side at last !

IV.

It was a City wondrous fair,

With precious walls—foundations sure.

No sounds of discord fell within ;

No sorrow there, nor death, 'nor sin.

No deep unquiet—no unrest ;

No partings come—no foes molest.

Within its walls earth's longings cease,

And ransomed souls have sweetest peace.

THE REST GIVER.

MATT. XI: 28.

Unrest through all the world within ;
Unquiet is the world without ;
Chidings and strife and tossing doubt—
Without, is storm ; within, is sin !

Above all outer storm and strife,
Meeting the wild unrest within,
And pressing back the hosts of sin,
A voice that bringeth a new life !

A point of rest—O see, my soul !
For every wound a healing balm ;

For every doubt the sweetest calm ;
The purest rest, and life's true goal.

'Tis He who once on Galilee
Bade stormy skies and sea, " Be still ;"
And both obeyed His sovereign will—
This rest for weary souls, 'tis He !

With Him, and every storm doth cease ;
As ship that touches longed for shore
With all its stormy voyage oer—
So in Him doth the soul find peace.

I hope to reach that stormless clime
Beyond the dark uncertainties,
Beyond the deep perplexities,
Beyond the fever heat of Time.

I hope to reach at last that Home

And see that Friend Divinely Fair,

And find soul-rest forever there

In grace of the Unchanging One!

ACCORD.

A World of wondrous build beyond the skies
Which God is filling with all harmonies.
And from all worlds sweet sounds to meet His
     ear ;
And God doth touch a Keyboard ever here.
Believing human hearts are living Keys
From which the Master brings forth harmonies.
He knows the " how," He knows the " when,"
     and " where "
To touch, to bring forth strains surpassing fair.
And like a skillful Player He doth start
Most wondrous chords from each believing heart.
Low minor strains of sorrow tremble here ;

And lofty notes of gladness echo there !

Here goes one pilgrim with his plaintive song

Trudging with dusty feet earth's vales along.

And there with happy hymns on hill tops fair,

Another goes who scarcely knows a tear.

There seem to be harsh discords in this life ;

And words with words, and deeds with deeds at
  strife.

But to His ear, whose hand doth touch the keys,

All come and blend in wondrous harmonies.

And mingled thus, all faith in anthem sweet,

Like incense rises to the Mercy Seat.

So Life, however humble, lowly, sad,

Still has some note to make the Master glad.

There is a chorus in Eternity

With which true Life is in sweet harmony.

And when the *finale* of this life is given

'Twill but enlarge the chorus there in Heaven !

WISE OR FOOLISH?

I.

Is this man wise or foolish?

    Frosts are the earth forsaking ;

    Spring, Winter's place is taking ;

    Where e'er your feet are straying,

    Blossoms and buds are saying :

        " Spring, Winter's place is taking."

Is this man wise or foolish?

    The orchard blooms possessing

    The air with fragrant blessing

    The wind from boughs are shaking ;—

Fruit germs their places taking,
    A Harvest-Prophet making !

Is this man wise or foolish ?
    He plucks the germs in hunger ;
    Nor can he wait till longer
    The tree shall feed and nourish ;—
    Air, sun and rain shall cherish
        Germs into fruit for hunger.

Is this man wise or foolish ?
    Germs stay not hungry craving !
    An orchard full there having,
    On sapless nothings feeding,
    As much as ever needing !—
       · Green germs feed not our craving !

Is this man wise or foolish ?
    The boughs no fruitage bringing —

No golden apples clinging.

The man, still, food is needing :

Desires and nothing feeding—

    Germs gone, no fruitage bringing !

Is this man wise or foolish ?—

    To pluck the buds in forming

    And have no fruit adorning ?

    Now useless—no *Then* bringing !

    Hunger forever clinging—

        Buds plucked—no fruitage forming!

II.

Is this man wise or foolish ?

    The soul's Spring-time abusing—

    This life for soul-wants using !

    Plucking the germs, and trying

    To feed a soul undying—

        The Spring-time buds abusing !

Is this man wise or foolish?

> This life thus used no blessing
> For souls is here possessing;
> Robbed here no fruitage bringing—
> No golden apples clinging—
>> Up there, no harvest blessing.

Is this man wise or foolish?

> Can droppings fill an ocean?
> Can Time stay the commotion
> Of endless soul-wants, needing
> Eternity for feeding?
>> Can droppings fill an ocean?

Is this man wise or foolish?

> All hope of fruit forsaking;
> A tasteless nothing taking.
> In Spring his Harvest using—

Eternity abusing !—

    Germs for the harvest taking !

Oh ! to be wise, not foolish !

    This life is here possessing

    A great and harvest blessing.

    Germs spared, ripe fruit is clinging ;

    Time spared, our Heaven is bringing.

      Spring-time is richest blessing !

LISTENING.

I've heard it said that Nature's untamed child,
Far out upon the Prairie's fenceless wild,
When the approach of foot-beat he would hear
Bends to the earth his wary, listening ear;
And soon on unseen train the sound is heard,
And not the frailest grass or flower is stirred.

The Universal Voice some cannot hear
Till Sorrow bends to earth the soul's sad ear.
And he who would the sweetest accents know
Must, humble hearted, bend and listen low.
Then, like the chimes of steeple towering high
And sprinkling with its blessings passers by,

The soul that listens with a humble care
Hears wondrous music in the Upper Air!

There is along a foreign rocky shore
In mountain fastness near the ocean's roar,
A giant harp whose strings are iron bands
Strung high from cliff to cliff by skillful hands.
When skies are clear and trees are windless,
        when
No stir is on the mountain or in glen,
In calm bright days or starry nights, around
The mountain harp gives forth no slightest sound.
But when the storm awakes oer sea and land
Euroclydon's dread fingers strike each strand,
And music fills the glen and wakes the shore,
Swelling high over all the stormy roar!

Some souls in calms and happiness are still;
No sounds resound on ocean, shore or hill!

Prosperity is far too weak a thing to be

Musician to a soul like boundless sea!

From cliff to cliff within, God-strung, are strings

Of giant power where Tempest sits and sings!

When storms sweep through soul-glens and up
the shore

Blinded by foam and deafened by the roar,

The Hand Omnipotent strikes all the strings,

And mid the storm the sweetest music sings.

Adversity—Euroclydon—must be

The stern musician by such soul's vast sea!

When woods and hills are windless and have rest,

All music dies within such human breast.

Not all may stand like giants on the shore,

Joying and singing mid the wildest roar!

Some souls hear best, and sing when storms are
high,

But most souls listen best neath quiet sky.

Yet all Thy people, Lord, Thy voice shall hear ;

In ocean storms or in the quiet clear ;

In Goshen Land or by some dread Red Sea ;

In Sinai's thunder wierd with majesty,

Or down from wondrous heights of Calvary ;

By some brack Marah or at Elim palms ;

In battle storms or Canaan's restful calms.

As sandal-wood transports the fragrant breath

Of native forests past the axman's death,

And brings it down the ages till we meet

The sandal perfume on some foreign street ;

Our souls shall carry Thy sweet-promise, Lord,

And every echo of Thy fragrant Word

Far down the years, and oer the rapid River

Into the city of the great Forever.

We'll meet their fragrance when we sinless greet

Thee in the Walls along the Golden Street.

Listening to hear, and hearing to obey.

Bend low or stand erect and reach the day!

UNRAVELED.

I.

In the city of Rome in the Palace of Justice they
show you a chamber
Which artists of eld-time have frescoed with wonderful skill on the ceiling ;
And walls are the traceried fancies which seem
but a maze of confusion.
Fair Asphodels, planted by ancients for food for
the souls of departed—
And Amaranth blossoms foretelling the life that
will bloom on immortal—

And trees from the Naxian groves, seem all on
the ceiling transplanted ;

And, hanging along on the wainscot, full clusters from vineyards of Zantè.

You look, and the soft minster spires seem rising
and towering to Heaven ;

The sounds of the bells seem melodious in chimes
in the beautiful turrets.

The soul drinks the draught of confusion, as one
of the oxymel drinketh.

The bitter and sweet are so mingled—the light
and the dark are so jumbled,

The stranger at Rome in the Palace of Justice
can find but confusion ;

And the scales in the hand of the Statue seem
wavering far from the balance !

They lead you at length to a centre, and bid you
look round on the wonder !

Behold! from that spot all the paintings move out
into picture concordant.

The spires of the minster melodious seem chiming with exquisite sweetness—

And all that before was harsh discord, with harmonies Heavenly vibrate!

The Asphodels bloom from the grave-sod—the
Amaranths blossom in Glory—

The Naxian groves and the clusters of Zante
breathe fragrant with fruitage.

You see from that spot all the glory that lay in
the plan of the artists.

Each panel and deep-seated oriel—each touch of
the brush wears a meaning.

Like a green frescoed Paradise breaketh the
paintings in joy on your vision!

II.

In the World, God's wonderful Palace of Time,
  all seems in confusion.

Like Books of the Hebrews we're reading His
  wonders forevermore backward!

Far upward where God's starry islands are moored in the Infinite Ocean

We gaze, and the ceiling seems painted by hand
  of a blundering artist.

Adown the dim corridors Past, all History seems
  without meaning;

And if the soul saileth avoyaging into the waters
  Eternal,

The keel is soon grating on reef-rocks, or lost,
  by some hurricane driven!

And all that is called by man "knowing" is only
  the shadow of Knowledge!

We plant by the tomb the fair Asphodels, mourn-
    ing for spirits departed;

Our Amaranths, types of immortal, are withered
    this side the Eternal;

Our hopes, like the shafts of Acestes, are kindled
    and burned with their flying!

What artist hath frescoed this Palace—its walls,
    and its floors, and its ceiling?

What hand hath reared up these mountains like
    spires of some minster toward Heaven?

Who anchored the stars and the sun in the 'Infi-
    nite Ocean above us?

Who crowdeth the long caravan of beings across
    the bleak desert?

Who filleth the grave-yards, and maketh in souls
    an emptiness awful?

We drink in the draught as one drinketh the
    oxymel—bitter and sweetness.

The World, the vast Palace of God, seems full
of hints and confusion!

There is on a Hill-top a centre where, standing,
the soul sees a wonder!
The one alone spot of the World where the riddles of Time have solution—
The one alone spot of the Earth where God's
ways, elsewhere dark, have clear meaning!
There light falls on night, and the Future with
glory illumines the Present ;
The past up its corridors echoes the music that
makes Time accordant.
The Islands of God, the far stars, are worlds in
the deep Upper Ocean ;
The pictures along on Time's walls are a path to
the Land of Forever!
On Calvary's hill-top you stand by the foot of
the Cross of the Savior.

Our Asphodel blossoms grow tapers illuming the
  low silent City:
The hand of the Christ swingeth outward the
  doors of the tombs to the Future,
Till the tears we so bitterly shed are dried like
  tears of the children;
The Amaranth taketh the place of the Asphodel—night bringeth morrow!

Oh! wonderful visions I see, and wondrous the
  sounds from this Hill-top!
The Naxian groves are a desert compared with
  the Life-trees of Glory:
And all the sweet flowers one meets with who
  walks in the Tuscany valleys,
Or sees on the hills of fair Sharon, are not like
  the flowers of the Kingdom!
From turrets and spires of our God—from the
  harps and the choirs of the angels—

From all the melodious bell-towers which rise
from the streets of the City,

Sweet songs come and light like a flock of fair
birds upon Calvary's summit.

The iceberg of sorrow melts down in the Gulf-
Stream of God's love and pity.

From this spot I can see on Time's walls, and
floors, and the beautiful ceiling,

That like herdsman on Grampian Hills, or shepherd in Bethlehem meadows,

God's Providence leadeth, defendeth, and feedeth
the sheep of His pastures,

And snatcheth the lambs of His flock from the
jaws of the dark foe Abaddon!

As one sees from summit of Washington far rolling billows of hill-tops

As grand as the billows of ocean, and nearer the
loftiest heavens,

I gaze on the hill-tops beneath me, and see the
  wild waves of commotion

All marching in orderly phalanx toward shore,
  like the march of God's army!

Here the Past and the Now and the Then are
  woven in harmony vibrant;

And the Cross is the brush in the hand of Him,
  the Infinite Painter.

My soul sails unmoored from this landing, like
  ship on a voyage eternal—

Lit on her way oer the waters by light from the
  Light-house far streaming.

The anchor will drop far away in the Bay of the
  City Supernal!—

All the soft minster spires of God's love, on the
  Hill-top drop down sweetest music!

NO ROOM.

Jesus has come to Bethlehem.
No room for him in crowded Inn.

He visits earth again to-day ;
Who has a room for Jesus, say ?

Or are the rooms all full again,
As on that night in Bethlehem ?

What heart is ready, swept and clean,
To take the weary Master in ?

Not many rooms there seem to be
For him who died on Calvary.

Plenty for gain—doors open wide :
Plenty where pleasures may abide.

Rooms in the world for Pilates still ;
Rooms for the Pharisees to fill.

When Jesus knocketh at the door :
" Rooms are all full and late the hour."

Patient and loving, Jesus waits
Outside our hearts—outside our gates.

The Inn is full ; no room I see
For him who died on Calvary !

A manger some poor heart doth show,
Like Bethlehem of long ago.

Oh! make Him room. Turn out the sin
That crowds thy soul. Take Jesus in.

17

O Earth, give Jesus room, and He
Will change thy night to day for thee.

O give him room, tried, doubting heart,
And he will rest and peace impart.

Ye will *not* take this Stranger in ?
Earth still to Christ is Bethlehem.

No room in Life's thronged Inn I see
For him who died on Calvary.

WHO KNOWS?

They sailed under "orders sealed" far away—

 Who knows where their anchors will fall ?

Will it be by the shore in some quiet Bay ;

 Or under some bastion wall?

I stand on the wharf and gaze over the sea,

And yearn to find out what the voyage may be.

Some ship sailing homeward will tell me one day

If my loved ones are safe who have sailed thus

 away.

There's a sea where the "white caps" are toss-

 ing alway—

 Where the storms tack with sudden alarm—

Where you see no green hills shutting round a
　　safe Bay—
　　Who will keep all my loved ones from harm?
I stand on this wharf and gaze over this sea,
But never a ship comes with message to me.

Will no one e'er tell me the harbor they reach—
　　The souls of my loved ones whose sails
Went down on mine eyes? Did the bright Shin-
　　ing Beach
　　Greet their prows? or did the rough gales
Which sweep oer the sea wreck them all?　Are
　　they lost—
Shivered — shattered　forever　upon　the　Dark
　　Coast?

My heart beats alarm on the shores of this sea.
　　Scudding fiercely in offing, the sails
Are reefed not, and never a hand seems to be

On the helm—and the sea mad with gales!

Would God that some Seaman stood there on
the deck—

Would God that some power would save them
from wreck!

O sad Sea of Life with thy vast human fleet!

O that the safe Pilot may stand

At the wheel for my loved ones and help them to
meet

All the storms and bring them to land.

They are out of my sight in the tempest and
night—

Through the night may they sail in the Great
Master's sight.

NOT NOW BUT HEREAFTER.

JOHN XIII: 7.

There is a "Now," there is a "Then."

This side of life seems oft all vain,

A bundle of mere hints we gain!

      This shall not always be.

These contradictions at the most

Shall break on far Eternal Coast—

In the hereafter shall be lost!

      Sweet hope is this to me.

Darkness and clouds are round His throne ;

No paths through waters deep are known ;

No dimmest ray of light is shown
      Along my pilgrim road.
Unraveled mysteries are here ;
The mirage fills the marshy air.
Well, foul shall change to bright and fair,
      Up in the Land of God !

Along the earth-shores, sandy, low,
Waves rise and fall, tides ebb and flow ;
Hopes, in to-day—to-morrow go ;
      Mists, heavy oer Life's sea !
Hands outward stretched into the night !
Hearts ever yearning for the light ;
Eyes seeing, and yet lacking sight—
      This shall not always be !

Like printer's type, we often read
Inverted God's best, kindest deed.

Plain printed page these hearts much need,
  Our eyes so dimly see.
Hereafter, printed off, how kind
And plain will be what was so blind.
Not upside down, but right we'll find
  God's every act to be.

Our hearts up Tabors love to go.
Gethsemanes so dark and low
Our human feet tread sad and slow.
  "Why Lord, such hours?" we cry !
" The cup *I* give my child to thee ;
Canst thou not drink and trust to Me ?
Not now—hereafter thou shalt see,
  And know the reason why."

To weary hearts and sore, how kind
Such fountains by the way to find !

What healing for our eyes so blind !

    " What *I* do thou shalt see :

Not now—not here ; but thou shalt know

Why waters oft do overflow—

Why through such thorny maze must go

    The Life-way here for thee !"

O blessed day to dawn at last !

The sun no shadows more to cast—

All doubts forever to be past,

    In God's bright land above.

No veil between the Porch and Place

Where Jesus shows completed grace ;

No longer " through a glass " that face

    To see, so full of love.

O blessed day when God shall show

The channels where our lives did flow—

The sharp escapes from deepest woe,

      By His Almighty hand!

Hereafter, if not now, we'll see

Amid the storms how wisely He

Stood at the wheel for you and me,

      Guiding us safe to land.

Trust thou, and rest. Christ is thy Guide;

On stormiest sea thy bark may ride.

Thou canst not see paths through the tide—

      He all the way doth know.

A little while and thou shalt be

At anchor in Eternity.

There—over there " is no more sea "—

      No tides to ebb or flow.

BLIND.

The mountain rivulets have no eyes—
Then how can they run and leap, who knows?
And the sure unfolding of fragrant rose
Is ever to me a sweet surprise.

For the flowers see not the dawn of day—
Then how they can open their cups, who'll tell?
Each "morning-glory" and down hanging "bell"
Unfolds its leaflets in wondrous way.

The seed under ground—say, can that see?
And how does it know then the path to the sun?
And the way the dumb creatures from danger run
Is a matter of strange surprise to me!

The stars are blind, yet wheel through the air ;
For the birds and the leaflets I see no guide.
Creation is moving on every side—
Has some Great Ruler somewhere a care ?

The rivulets never lose their way ;
The flowers and blind grasses—they never forget;
Was there ever in leaflets a spirit to fret ?
And the birds greet surely the coming day.

The human soul can trust then, and rest.
He will see for the soul who sees for the leaves.
The pathway is certain to him who believes ;
And it leads the feet to the Land of the Blest.

REBUKE.

All days are sodden and drear, I said.

The sun is an exile far away ;

The leaves are crisp, and the flowers are dead ;

The skies are so cold and distant—I said.

    I looked :—the sun shone overhead ;

    The waters were smiling in placid Bay,

    The flowers were blooming, which seemed

        so dead ;

    And new life darted across my way.

The sea is ever unquiet—unkind !

The ships will never anchor, I said.

And the broken spars by the stormy wind,

And wrecks are all it leaveth behind.

> I looked :— where *was* the wild stormy
> wind ?
>
> The white wings flapped just overhead ?
>
> The pathless voyage was far behind,
>
> And Harbor-quiet was just ahead.

This life is valueless all, I said.

The good and the resting is far away.

My hopes are crisp and my effort is dead,

And all my Life-labor is failure, I said.

> I looked :—the green Hills were rising
> ahead ;
>
> And, sheltered and bright, a fair City of
> Day.
>
> "Reef sails—cast anchor," a sweet voice
> said.
>
> I'm anchored within the wide Heavenly
> Bay !

All deeds of the earth I did for Him

Who ruleth this City of the Skies,

Like ships of the sea come in—glide in

From the stormy waves and the shadows dim--

Yea, all that I strove to do for Him.

    I said:—no human effort e'er dies,

    But out from the earth's dark sea of sin

    It sails to the City in uppermost skies !

ALL THINGS.

ROM. VIII:28.

These human hearts are frail and feeble things—
Like fragile lutes which smallest touch unstrings.
In sunshine and in joy they seem in tune ;
The sun goes down oft times at highest noon.

Like Hebrews in a stranger land, so we
Weep sore by Rivers of Adversity ;
Yet God by Babel stream was guiding still
E'en Captive Jews to learn His righteous will.

Our sorrows, as our joys, are teachers true ;
And human hearts, though sore, have work to do.

Through light and shadows, through the dark and
     bright,
Life's pathway runs up to the Land of Light.
O'er mountains high, through valleys deep, it
     lies—
This Way of God to reach the lofty skies.

Our human eyes in darkness cannot see ;
The hill-tops high shut out the Land of Day.
There needs must be some places on Life's road
Where human eyes see not the Land of God !
Yet in the valleys, as on loftiest hill,
We journey Heavenward and obey his will.
And in the night and shadows still we be
Along God's road, as in the fairest day.

Rough work—sharp tools to polish diamonds
     bright:
18

Sharp tools to make dull hearts reflect God's
    light.
Between the upper and the nether grindstones,
    see
The wheat to flour is crushed, man's life to be.
The " mills of God grind close " but never fail:
No soul imperfect comes from out God's mill !
The husbandman with keenest, sharpest blade,
Fruit-bearing vines, instead of fruitless, made.
The artist takes a block of senseless stone—
Patient and skillful marks his lines upon ;
With little mallet strokes his work is done ;
An angel form instead of senseless stone !

God, like a skillful Artist, in great love
Fits our rough hearts for Heavenly seats above.
Material, shapeless, sinful souls He takes,
And living stones for Heavenly Temple makes.

Sharp chisel's ring, and many a mallet blow

Are heard within God's Quarry here below.

But patiently, and with a Master hand, works on

The Heavenly Artist till the work is done.

A ransomed soul comes forth God's work to
   praise,

Reflecting His rich love through endless days.

All tools of iron—all hammer strokes but tell

That when God works, and where, God works
   all well!

YE DINNA KEN.

Ye watna when His voice may ca'—
Maist onie time—" maist onie day ; "
Frae yont the skies aboon may fa'
Heaven's cantie licht athwart thy way.
　　It may be soon—it winna be lang,
　　For the life steps doun a steep hill gang.

It may be that the way will end
Amid the day-dawn's glad surprise,
Where softest speechless glories blend
The bonnie hues o' Paradise.
　　It may be soon—it winna be lang,
　　For the life-steps doun a steep hill gang.

Or He may ca' at noon o' nicht—

I 'll hae my lamp wi' oil at han' ;

I 'll hae it trimmed an' burnin' bricht,

Like ane who waits his Lord's comman'.

  It may be soon—it winna be lang,

  For the life steps doun a steep hill gang.

Or on the highest hills o'day

The years o' Time may fin' an en'.

It winna fash—for wha wad say

That Time is mon's maist cherished frien' ?

  It may be soon—it winna be lang,

  For the life steps doun a steep hill gang.

Ye dinna ken—the cry may fa'

Maist onie time—" maist onie day."

We winna strae frae richt awa'—

In lanes o' sin ane should na stay.

  It may be soon—it winna be lang,

  For the life steps doun a steep hill gang.

I ken the refluent sea o' Life
Wi' sluggish 'waters greets the shore.
I 'll fin' a sweet surcease o' strife—
Woes ebb to flow again nae more.

  It may be soon—it winna be lang,

  For the life steps doun a steep hill gang.

My soul like oarsman lang hae pu'ed
Wi' face to shore and back to sea,
And a' God's ways misunderstood—
Ah weel! this winna always be!

  It may be soon—it winna be lang,

  For the life steps doun a steep hill gang.

O wha can ken? Our wark maun be
To keep the household clean and braw ;
That when He comes He winna see
The servant frae his post awa'.

  It may be soon—it winna be lang,

  For the life steps doun a steep hill gang.

The Gowden Gate may unco soon
Swing back and show the Gowden Street !
The frien's, the cheer, the home aboon
Maist onie time our souls may greet.

> It may be soon—it winna be lang,
> For the life steps doun a steep hill gang.

Ilk dissonant clangor o' the warl'--
A' sailing shades cast dark by sin
Will pass—and a' Time's staining marl—
And sang Redeemed sing begin.

> It may be soon—it winna be lang,
> For the life steps doun a steep hill gang.

Let 's kindle lamps and mak them burn
Wi' good fresh oil and keep them bricht.
I canna say but I discern
Ayont the coming form o' nicht.

> It may be soon—it winna be lang,
> For the life steps doun a steep hill gang.

But a' His bairns shall climb the height

That rins frae Death-stream up the way

Where softest glimmering o' Heaven's light

May greet the soul " maist onie day."

    It may be soon—it winna be lang,

    For the life steps doun a steep hill gang.

BE TRUE.

While strength is given to do for God,
While I may reap the rich ripe grain,
Must I give way to sense of pain
That comes to meet me on the road,
And let the days drift on in vain?

Must I grow weary—must I faint
While day is mine and sun doth shine,
And doors swing wide for work Divine?
And shall I utter harsh complaint—
Sit down and murmur and repine?

I know there come along Life's way

Dark sodden days and beating rain ;

There needs must be some throbbing pain—

Its form may meet me any day.

But harvest wastes !   Time reaps the grain !

Because of sorrow yet to be

I will not slacken pace, nor rest.

He meeteth Sorrow's form the best

Who keeps eyes on Eternity,

And reapeth God's Time-fields the best !

For duty done in faith and love,

Like Heavenly Alchemist, can take

This common life and new life make

Fit to be lived in Land above.

Be true, my soul, for Truth's sweet sake !

RESURGAM.

When the Winter of waiting shall burst into
    Spring,
And the seed in "God's Acres," the grave-yards,
    shall rise,
Can any one tell if His power then will bring
The friends that we know—that we love to our
    eyes?
        Or up in the Heavenly Places
        Shall we greet only cold stranger faces?

Why God, here below, when each Winter is past,
Brings the lilies and roses—the flowers that we
    know,

Some one tell us!—why does He not cast

Strange comers to greet us from robes of the

    snow ?

        Is it prophecy soothingly spoken

        To hearts that with sorrow are broken ?

When the wheat brings us corn, and sharp this-

    tles appear

Where grape-vines are planted ; when figs meet

    our eyes

On bushes of bramble, our hearts then may fear

That stranger shall greet us for loved one who

    dies !—

        That we'll meet only cold stranger faces

        Up there in the Heavenly Places.

Oh! when the cold Winter called " Death" is

    behind,

And Spring-time of vast Resurrection appears,

I am sure that our hearts, in God's gardens, shall
  find
All the flowers which the love of the earth-time
  endears.
  He will give us the old lovely faces
  Up there in the new Heavenly Places.

And the dying is only the sailing away
Of the habitant over the sea to the shore
Where the gloom of the storm-night breaks into
  the day—
Where one hears the reefs moaning with sorrow
  no more.
  When we meet in the bright Heavenly
  Places,
  We shall greet all the sweet, long-lost
  faces !

LIFE.

I.

A ship lies moored to the shore,

With its anchor deep in sand.

The useless sails are windless overhead ;

The decks are hushed as City of the Dead ;

And in the offing, billowy waters o'er,

Fair vessels glide apast on every hand.

I cannot cut the shore-bound line ;

The anchor's weight I cannot weigh !

The East-wind stoutly pulls my sail ;

The West-wind blows a stormy gale.

"All the other ships can glide to sea—

But shore-lines and anchors are for me."

I fret and I pine with my nerveless will,

Anchored and moored to the shore all still !

II.

The ship bounds over the wave.

What hand can steady the helm ?

Euroclydon is beating overhead ;

Caverns of Ocean cry, with all their dead.

My eyes seek Heaven in vain for star to save.

Storm-terrors all my being overwhelm !

Oh ! how I long to anchor by some shore !

I feel so lost amid this wild uproar,

I scarce can think that God's all-hearing ear

My feeble pleading cries for help can hear.

I'm far away, adrift, and driven and lost ;

Anchorless, helmless, mastless, tempest-tossed !

III.

The ship grates harsh on the sand,

And crashes along some shore!

I shut my eyes and sink beneath the wave,

And sinking cry: "O Master, wake and save."

Nothing but spars and broken masts at hand;

And in mine ears the ocean's ceaseless roar!—

What silence here beneath such stormy sea!

What peaceful quiet comes at last to me!

The fret and wave-surf of the upper-deep

This bottom silence lulls to wakeless sleep.

Downward seems upward: depths seem heights:
     to die

Seems Royal Road up to the Hills and Sky.

And stormiest hour when all seems wrecked and
     lost,

Is where the ship the Harbor Bar has crossed.

IV.

The ship is moored at the shore,

And anchored safe at the land.

How blest this Harbor far beyond that sea ;

These Hills of God, how breezy, fair and free !

The soul sails here its frail light bark no more ;

No more strikes rocks, or rasps along the sand.

How clearly now I see the pilot steer

Through stormy waters—through the calm and

    clear.

How plain to me that mooring far behind

At life's fair dawn was meant for wise and kind.

Drifting and wreck and anchorage were planned

To lead me here to this sweet Heavenly Land :—

Here to this Harbor neath Celestial Hill :—

Here to this City where all storms are still.

COMPENSATION.

Oft hitherto have my strange days
Inwound through many a doubtful maze,
And crept through strangely devious ways.

Now oer Life's hills and levels lone ;
Green fields and woodlands overgrown :
Or where deep waters pulse and moan.

Now neath the blessed sunshine free :
Oer breezy moors of liberty :
Neath skies outpouring melody.

By palace wall or haunted tomb ;

Through light and shadow—joy and gloom—
My life has known both blight and bloom.

Now here, as from some mountain height,
Oer all Life's path I strain my sight—
And lo ! the dark turns into light.

Oer all Life's mists—cold, dim and chill—
Through heart and soul with sweetest thrill,
A voice is saying : " Peace, be still."

COMING IN.

JOHN, LAST CHAPTER.

I.

'Twas a weary night on Galilee;

The fisherman's boat swung lazily;

The nets hung empty; the slow-swung oar

Like Disappointment was seeking the shore.

The gloam of the day outlined the land;

Hush held the forests on every hand;

The Mountains of Moab rose far away;

And over Gennesar the dawning lay.

The Star of Morning crowns Bashan Hills;

The snow on Hermon the North-sky fills;

The shore is silent as Galilee ;
The waves are as silent as Silence can be.

The Star of Bashan has paled away ;
The snows of Hermon have greeted the day ;
The fisherman's boat swings nearer the land ;
And a Form all glorious along the strand.

The Christ arisen ! The Christ—tis He
At early dawning by Galilee.
The night all weary flies fast away ;
The wavering shadows quick turn to day.

II.

And after dragging my nets at sea,
And after toiling on Galilee,
With nets still empty, my weary oar
With weary swinging is seeking the shore.

I read this chapter :—on every hand

The still gray morning outlines the land ;

The Mountains of Moab rise far away ;

And over Gennesar breaks quiet day.

And over my sorrows hangs Bashan Star ;

And snowy Hermon gleams out afar ;

Soul-shore is silent as Galilee ;

My heart is as waveless as sea can be.

And while I'm reading my boat nears land.

O form of Jesus along the strand !

O voice of Jesus that comes to me !

O blessed dawning on Galilee !

The sweet last chapter—I read it through.

Its tender verses refresh like dew ;

My oar-swing quickens—I soon touch land,

And feast with Jesus along the strand.

I think now often on Seas of Care

Of beautiful verses where Day-springs are ;

And over Gennesar the Day-star springs,

And lights with its glory all earthly things.

III.

'Twas a weary night on Galilee—

A night of toiling to you and me.

Our nets hung empty, our weary oar

Swung wearily nearing the far off Shore.

But at the dawning what Quiet Land !

What hills and mountains before us stand !

The Mountains of Glory rose far away,

And over the Harbor what stillness lay !

And after dragging our nets at sea ;

And after toiling on Galilee,

Oh ! Hills Celestial that rise so fair—

Oh ! City the Golden along the air !

And Jesus is standing upon the shore—
The same sweet Jesus of days of yore:
By Gennesar of Time or Eternity,
The same sweet Jesus to you and me.

LANDING.

ACTS XXVII. 27.

Twas the midnight of storm
    By the Island's rough shore,
When the quick, sharp alarm
    Of the water's dull roar
Surging harsh on the strand
    Wakened gloomiest fear!
And they deemed that the land
    Of some country was near!

As seaman can tell
    By the weeds floating by,
Or the land-birds which swell
    On the blasts of the sky;

That dull splash and roar
    Of the waves on the ear
Tell the sailors the shore
    Of some country is near !

So they dropped down the lead
    On the fast shelving shore—
And they found with great dread
    That it shelved more and more !
So their anchors they cast
    In the depths of despair ;
For the deep seas are past,
    And some country is near.

But the servant of God
    Sailed on Adria's wave ;
And the Master there rode
    On the midnight to save.
And with God on the blast

No seaman need fear
Though the breakers' harsh dash
　　Tells some country is near.

When the midnight was past,
　　And the dawning was nigh,
The seamen descried
　　Rough Malta close by.
They cut anchors sharp,
　　And pushed on in fear,
And they drave toward the strand
　　Of the country so near !

The seamen and he
　　Whom the Lord would save passed
Safe in from the sea
　　To the Island at last.
Touched the shore—safely there
　　In from wreck and from fear !

No more in despair
　　On the country once near!

II.

O souls that do sail
　　On the dark stormy sea,
Drop the lead mid the gale,
　　And find out where ye be!
If ye hark, some dull roar
　　May fall on your ear,
Of the waves on the shore
　　Of some country that's near.

As tired seamen do greet
　　The land-bird's swift wing;
Or gladly do meet
　　The sea-weed's green swing,
Shall souls not rejoice
　　When the sounds echo clear,

Which tell by their voice

 That some country is near?

There! Sounds the low rote

 Of the waves on the shore!

As nearer I float,

 It beats more and more!

I sound: "Fathoms twenty:"

 "Fifteen"—There! I hear

The tokens, quick, plenty,

 Of some country that's near!

Tis midnight! Loud dashing

 The waves beat the strand!

I catch the quick splashing

 On some shore at hand.

My soul, shall we perish?

 But why should we fear?

What sweet hopes we cherish

Of some country that's near !

Our God can control
    Every storm on the sea.
Where the loud billows roll
    He is sailing with thee !
On Malta's rough landing
    No waves' dash I hear !
No danger of stranding
    On this country that's near.

When Death's night drives past,
    And Life's dawning 's at hand,
Our anchors we'll cast
    In the Bay at the land.
O beautiful Harbor !
    O skies blue and clear !
My soul greets the splendor
    Of the country that's near !

Each soul shall yet glide

    From the storm and the wave,

If Life's sea he doth ride

    With the Lord who can save.

No night, and no storm,

    And no foe, and no fear

Can wreck souls, or drift

    From the country that's near!

So soul, let us sound!

    On the dark midnight sea

Watch the sounds that abound,

    And learn where we be.

By the fast shelving shore—

    By the land-signs so clear,

We may learn more and more

    That some country is near.

There see! The green hill tops

Beyond us arise.

There hark! every reef-note

Of sea-dangers dies.

Some souls to spars clinging—

Some through the surf cast—

All, clinging to Jesus,

Have landed at last.

Milton Keynes UK
Ingram Content Group UK Ltd.
UKHW010637270324
440147UK00003B/67

9 783385 383647